The Money-Raising
Nonprofit Brand

The Money-Raising Nonprofit Brand

Motivating Donors to Give, Give Happily, and Keep on Giving

Jeff Brooks

WILEY

Contents

PART TWO
Your Call to Action

*How Your Cause Connects with Donors and Brings
Your Brand into Their Lives*

CONTENTS

CONTENTS

Acknowledgments

Thank you to my excellent clients and colleagues at TrueSense Marketing. You've given me the opportunity to observe and shape nonprofit brands, and you've challenged my thinking on what works and what doesn't. Thanks also to the wonderful cafés of Seattle's Pioneer Square and Queen Anne Hill, whose caffeine and ambience enabled much of the writing of this book.

About the Author

Jeff Brooks, creative director at TrueSense Marketing, has served the nonprofit community for more than 25 years, working as a writer and creative director on behalf of top North American nonprofits, including CARE, St. Jude Children's Research Hospital, World Vision, Feeding America, World Relief, and dozens of urban rescue missions and Salvation Army divisions. He has planned and executed hundreds of campaigns in direct mail, print, radio, the Internet, and other media that have motivated millions of donors to help make the world a better place. He blogs at futurefundraisingnow.com, podcasts at fundraisingisbeautiful. com, and is the author of the popular book *The Fundraiser's Guide to Irresistible Communications* (2012). He lives in Seattle.

Introduction

How This Book Can Transform Your Fundraising

"We are rebranding."

Every time I hear those three words, I half-expect a sudden minor chord, the kind you hear in old movies when someone mentions the villain's name.

I wish that chord were audible. Then I could say—darkly, like a supporting character who's probably doomed—"I have a bad feeling about this." That would at least bring a film noir drama to the situation, which would have to be better than the dreary and discouraging way rebranding usually goes.

"We are rebranding" should mean something like this: *We're going to make systemic changes to the way we connect with the outside world that will help people understand and love our cause. This will improve our fundraising.*

If only.

Instead, "We are rebranding" at a nonprofit usually means something more like this: *We face one to three years of painfully weak fundraising results. A lot of revenue will be lost, and a number of people will be fired.*

It's not just me. Almost anyone who serves the nonprofit sector as a fundraising consultant or agency professional will back me up: That's the ugly course rebranding usually follows.

If every time you tuned your car radio to an AM station your right rear wheel fell off, you'd eventually come to the conclusion that the AM radio and the right rear wheel were connected. You might start to perceive your AM radio as a terrible piece of equipment that you should never, ever use.

Many of the best professionals in fundraising long ago came to the conclusion that *branding is a force for evil*—that you can have brand, or fundraising, but you can never have both. We need to change that. Because we can't afford to ignore branding. It's far too important.

• • •

I know a guy who collects news accounts of injuries and deaths caused by forklift accidents. He has so many of these stories, he has almost come to believe that forklifts are enemies of the human race. It's as if he's in a bad horror movie from the 1950s, one that ends with the camera pulling back to reveal the city sidewalks thronged with forklifts—and no humans. (Cue scary closing credits music.)

Let's get real: Forklifts are not evil. They're useful machines. Sometimes, something goes wrong with a forklift and someone gets hurt. To my knowledge, it's human error every time.

Branding is that way, too.

Those "branding accidents" are the equivalent of forklifts knocking over stacks of crates or backing off loading docks. It's not the forklifts' fault—it's people wrongly or clumsily operating a powerful tool.

Nonprofit fundraising is like a big warehouse full of forklifts being driven by pretty much anyone who feels like driving one. No certification or training is required. That leads to a lot of accidents.

To make matters worse, people keep hiring fighter-jet pilots to show them how to drive forklifts. These pilots' sense of speed and altitude is radically misaligned with the capabilities of forklifts—and they don't recognize the problem. With predictable results.

Before I take this metaphor so far we can't drag it back,[1] I have good news for you: *There's another way to do nonprofit branding.* You can build a great brand that won't land you in a horror-movie scenario, but instead measurably boost your fundraising metrics. That includes bottom-line revenue.

This book will show you how, and that's how you'll transform your fundraising.

---

1. As you'll notice throughout this book, I enjoy metaphors.

Think of this book as a training manual for forklift drivers—that is, nonprofit brand builders who need to raise funds. That's you if you are in one of these groups:

- Fundraising or marketing professionals working at a nonprofit organization.

- Leaders or board members who want to provide meaningful leadership to the fundraisers in your organization.

- Agency professionals or consultants who serve nonprofits and want to help clients achieve breakthrough fundraising results.

- Anyone who wants to join the fundraising profession well equipped and clear-eyed about the challenges you'll face.

You'll find a realistic and experienced guide that will help you use the powerful tool of branding.

• • •

Until recently, I was one of those fundraising people who thought branding was evil. That was my best explanation for the repeated branding accidents I saw—the organizations that faced crippling losses of revenue and the derailed careers that resulted. What I didn't know was that I was making the same error as my friend who collects forklift stories. My attitude changed after I witnessed up-close several cases where nonprofit branding helped fundraising *soar*.

I started to pay close attention to the practices of successful fundraisers who made their brands work for them and not against them. I studied my own clients—where I typically have a lot of inside information—as well as organizations I could only observe from their public activities. I asked a lot of people a lot of questions.

A coherent pattern started to appear. The brands that correlated with successful fundraising had characteristics in common—and they were strikingly different from the commercial brands we know, admire, and often try to imitate.

A light turned on for me: Simply applying the principles of commercial branding to nonprofit fundraising is exactly the wrong thing to do. It's the cause of most branding accidents.

But getting it right, building your brand the way successful fundraisers do, will help you motivate donors to give, give happily, and keep on giving.

Your brand can—and should—do that for you.

THE MONEY-RAISING NONPROFIT BRAND

This book is divided into four sections, each one meant to show you one piece of the nonprofit brand puzzle:

- The first section (Chapters 1 through 5) shows how and why nonprofit rebranding goes wrong when it's patterned after commercial-style branding—when a cavalier disregard for what we know about donors and their motivations is combined with commercial expertise. You'll also learn how much an ill-conceived rebranding is likely to cost you in lost fundraising revenue.

- The second section (Chapters 6 through 9) is about the first and most important characteristic of a Money-Raising Nonprofit Brand: a clear and compelling call to action that shows donors what they can do to make the world a better place through your organization.

- The third section (Chapters 9 and 10) is about the correct use of images to connect with donors and raise funds. It's your "fundraising icon," a specific use of image that powers the effectiveness of the Money-Raising Nonprofit Brand.

- The fourth section (Chapters 11 through 14) is about how a Money-Raising Nonprofit Brand has donor-focused systems and culture. When you focus on your donors, you give them more reasons to get involved—and stay involved.

• • •

There are two more things you should know about this book and the brand-building advice it will give you:

1. I didn't invent this stuff. I wish I had, but every bit of it predates me. I'm describing the ways smart nonprofits connect with their donors and raise more money for their causes. Follow this advice, and you'll be in good company.

2. This it not an all-or-nothing "system." The parts of the Money-Raising Brand are not interdependent. If you *can't* do some part of what you find here, *do what you can*. You can still get meaningful improvements in your fundraising.

My hope for you, the nonprofit brand builder who wants to make a positive mark, is that as you read the following pages you'll get the same sense of enlightenment that I got when I discovered these things. I also hope you'll put these ideas to work and know the unparalleled joy that comes when you see your work unleash your donors' generosity more than ever before.

You—and your cause—deserve that.

The Money-Raising Nonprofit Brand

PART ONE

The Money-Losing
Nonprofit Brand

*How Branding Often Goes Wrong for
Nonprofit Organizations*

CHAPTER ONE

How and Why Commercial-Style Branding Can Torpedo Your Organization

Thinking about rebranding to improve your fundraising results? Think again. Commercial-style branding is the wrong tool for nonprofits. If you try to attach that type of brand to your organization, you can expect painful drops in revenue and engagement.

The Color Master held us in the palm of his manicured hand.

He was part of a team of Brand Experts who'd been flown in to hand down my client's new brand—a thing of beauty that would launch the organization into a new era of public visibility, sky-rocketing revenue, and cutting-edge design. (That's how an energetic memo from the VP of marketing put it.)

The audience of 50 or so "stakeholders" sat in a darkened meeting room, staring like goldfish at the Color Master's slides.

The stake I held was helping the organization produce its direct-mail and online fundraising. I was at this daylong seminar with experts from the branding agency to get my "marching orders" on how the new brand would play out in fundraising.

The screen showed a solid rectangle of purple.

"Warm Medium Eggplant," the Color Master said. None of his colors had regular names like "purple," and most of them had two adjectives. "Warm Medium Eggplant creates a sort of visual embrace." Long pause. "It makes you feel cozy and included. Like you're six years old and sitting in Grandma's kitchen. It evokes the aroma of baking—something delicious, with a hint of cardamom."

Everyone in the room swooned. All that from *purple*—excuse me—*Warm Medium Eggplant?*

"This is going to be a grand slam," someone behind me stage-whispered.

While I pondered what a "grand slam" might be for a color, images of purple things flashed by quickly on the screen. A thick purple blanket. Grapes. A teapot—old-fashioned, yet purple.

Then the screen went dark. The Color Master's face, floating above his black turtleneck, was the only visible thing in the room. "Warm Medium Eggplant," he intoned, "is our main primary accent color." That meant it was one of the two colors of the yet-to-be revealed new logo, and we would be required to use it in great abundance.

"Whoever would have dreamed of *purple?*" The stage whisperer asked from behind me. "It's so *creative.*"

I never would have dreamed of it, I thought. The organization was a venerable American institution that had been helping the poor for three generations. It owned a piece of psychological real estate that most fundraisers would give their firstborn to have: Its donors saw giving as a sign of patriotism. The old, soon-to-be-scrapped logo tapped into that perception: It was red, white, and blue, and included a stylized stars-and-stripes flag.

Reliable sources had it that the rebranding work was costing the organization $300,000. But hey, what's $300,000 when you consider the benefits the new brand was going to bring? According to the Brand Experts, we could look forward to:

- Paradigm-crushing improvements in awareness and revenue! (That's exactly how they put it.)

- Access to an elusive but promising new demographic of young, smart, affluent donors!

- An end to a dated look that was, frankly, a résumé stain for any self-respecting creative person!

The investment in the brand would more than pay off—tangibly and intangibly—before we knew it! (Also exactly how they put it.)

The screen became a block of yellow. A pale yellow, almost white. "Light Vibrant Butter," the Color Master intoned. He said it with such solemn drama that hearing God say "Let there be light" could hardly have been more arresting.

He told us how butter changes hue throughout the year with the diet of cows. In summer, when they're eating green grass, the butter is a darker yellow. In winter while they eat hay, the butter lightens up, almost to white. Light Vibrant Butter, the Color Master said, captures the color of butter after its palest winter hue when grass has just returned to the cows' diets.

Someone near the front of the room made the type of sound you give especially good fireworks displays: *Ooooh!* Honestly, the Color Master's presentation had earned that reaction. I wish all the business presentations I attend were half as well done.

We watched a series of pale yellow things on the screen. None of them was butter. He followed with a quicker tour of the rest of the palette. There was no flag red. No flag blue. There was a bluish gray called Montana Pine Smoke.

After the Color Master, the presentation went downhill. He was clearly the star player on the team of Brand Experts.

The Font Guy spoke in a soft monotone. He avoided eye contact, preferring to turn to us and look at his own slides on the screen, which was behind and above him. His big reveal was the new brand font: I'll call it Unreadable Sans, along with its sidekick, Unreadable Sans Extra—tall, anorexic fonts. The ascenders were extra-long, while the descenders were oddly short, as if afraid to venture too far from their letters. For most fonts, the word "extra" means bold. For Unreadable Sans, it meant extra thin.

"This font will really catch fire," the Font Guy muttered, "when you reverse it against Medium Warm Eggplant." The idea of flaming type captured my imagination, so I couldn't focus on him any further.

Next up was the Imagist. She would have been called a photographer most places, but the executive who introduced her pointed out that she was no mere shutterbug: She'd had work exhibited in the Museum of Modern Art. He didn't say which Museum of Modern Art.

The Imagist's guidelines for photography under the new brand boiled down to this: We were always to show beautiful, happy children in multiracial groups of three to eight, all of them wearing colors that matched the new palette. A sad, fearful, or even pensive face would undermine the charity's Brand Promise, which was "hope."

That's right—the entire promise had been boiled down to one word: *Hope*.

The happy children in the photos were always to be cut out from their surroundings and set against backgrounds of Medium Warm Eggplant or Light Vibrant Butter—to avoid the possibility of revealing any squalor, poverty, or other signs of hopelessness that might be lurking in the real world behind them.

Finally, the Wordsmith stepped up to the podium. He was pale and seemed to be in a constant state of flinching—clearly the lowest in the hierarchy of the Brand Experts. In their world, words are an afterthought. Color, font, and images do the real work.

His only thunder had been stolen by the Imagist when she revealed the Brand Promise, "Hope."

The Wordsmith's hands shook when he held up a copy of the new communications standards document. Among the new rules for copy were that we were required to say "food insecurity" rather than "hungry," and "marginalized" instead of "poor." Those tired old terms undercut the dignity of those the organization served, and were "not up to the standards of a modern brand." The Wordsmith briefly smiled while he said that last phrase. I suppose he considered it some of his best work.

He went on to explain that all marketing and fundraising materials must use the word *hope* as often as possible. But it should never be used as a verb, as in *They hope someone like you will help them*—because that would be "hokey." The brand promise would achieve its full power only as a conceptual noun.

Even the stage whisperer sounded unconvinced. He made a sound like "Yuh"—it might have been "Yeah," but it sounded more like "Yuck."

Before the tide of unbelief could rise, they brought out their big finish: the logo. The Color Master stepped back up to the podium with his personal cloud of charisma to show the logo: the organization's name, set in Unreadable Sans, colored Medium Warm Eggplant and Light Vibrant Butter. He assured us that minute adjustments—invisible to all but the most advanced type experts—had been made to the font to increase the visual impact.

"Up to date!" someone said from the back of the room. The Color Master gave us a thumbs-up, and applause rippled across the room. "Let's bring this puppy to life!" he said, and showed us images of the logo on a key fob, a baseball cap, the Times Square Jumbotron, a white Mini Cooper, and the screen of an iPad. No envelopes, letterhead, or reply forms. This logo existed for everything *but* direct mail.

That didn't mean they'd entirely forgotten the idea of getting donors. He showed a full-page ad designed to run in high-end magazines like *Vogue* and *GQ*. It was the word *hope*, reversed out against a page of Medium Warm Eggplant. The new logo sat in the lower right corner, and below that, much smaller, the organization's URL. Space had already been bought in upcoming issues. We could expect an influx of new donors—wealthy, urban, cool people like you and me and our friends.

Then the Color Master started to show the redesigned web site. The moment I saw the reversed-out word *hope* dominating the home page, I fled. I didn't wait for an elevator, but took the stairs 22 floors down to the ground. I wasn't ready to talk to anyone because I needed to think about the uncertain future my client's fundraising faced.

Out on the sidewalk, I turned my back to a stiff wind and started walking. I ran through the changes that had just been mandated:

- We no longer had the patriotic flag logo.

- The new colors were basically black and white, but more expensive and difficult to work with. Beyond that, we were now required to stay within a color palette of cold, dusty colors, most of which would reproduce poorly in four-color process printing—which, unless you're the royal family of a first-world nation, is how you print all fundraising materials.

- We were required to use fonts that became almost unreadable at anything more than eight words or smaller than 24-point size.

- The photo guidelines outlawed the entire class of images that were integral to every successful fundraising campaign we'd ever done—sad-eyed children who compelled compassion in anyone who looked at them. Now it was beautiful, untroubled children who showed no need for help.

- No one had ever put the old Brand Promise in writing, but if they had, it would have been something like *Be a good American and help fellow Americans in need.* Now we had a Brand Promise in writing: Hope. A one-word abstraction. Not only an abstraction, but an overused one.

- And the one-word magazine ad campaign? I already knew how that was going to turn out. You can't raise funds with one word. Unless that word is *earthquake* and there's been a catastrophic earthquake in the last 48 hours. Even then, you need a few more words plus a picture or two.

Almost everything anyone had ever done to raise funds for the organization was now in violation of the new brand standards.

The coming year was now a blank fundraising calendar. With no proven performers, we needed to invent new messages from beginning to end. A normal fundraising schedule changes and grows from year to year. It typically has a mix of winners, decent projects you're working to improve, and a few fatigued projects that you need to repair or replace. Our new schedule had no winners, no decent performers to improve. Just question marks. If you know fundraising, you know that most new ideas don't fly the first time you try them. Success comes from trying a lot of ideas and building on the better ones, while you trash the ones that don't work. We were suddenly floating free, no winners to work with. And no idea in what direction to seek success. Our only guidance: the new brand standards, which eliminated the approaches most likely to work.

Millions of dollars in revenue were now at risk. A string of weaker fundraising campaigns would hit the bottom line immediately. The cumulative impact would be collapsing donor retention as donors failed to respond. Every time a donor doesn't give, she moves closer to leaving your file forever. This meant years of famine ahead of us, even if we learned at miraculous speed how to make the new brand work.

A snowball's chance in hell? That theoretical snowball has more reasons for optimism than our fundraising program did that day.

Of course, that's not how the Brand Experts saw it. Their conception of what they'd done was this: They'd tossed aside a tired old marketing scheme that barely worked. The brilliance of the new brand virtually guaranteed dramatic improvements. The organization was in the midst of some of the healthiest fundraising growth in its history, but they dismissed that. It was nothing compared to what they were about to bring to life. They were sure they could leap-frog recent years of success and learning. They were young and optimistic.

Later on, I'll show you how things went after the new brand launched. But here's the one-sentence summary:

The new brand was a revenue disaster.

(It wasn't as bad as it might have been: The organization made some key compromises about rolling out the brand that protected a lot of revenue. More on that later, too.)

The most disturbing thing about this story is that I could tell it several times over. The details would differ, but the outcome is the same each time: Exciting new brand rolls out, followed by a damaging drop in fundraising revenue. If you've been in the fund-raising business for a while, you've probably seen it, too.

Brand Experts show up on their white horses, promising trans-formation. Then they heedlessly change almost everything that worked, and replace it all with cool new ideas that have never been exposed to the donor marketplace. It takes a special form of ignorance—the kind that's common among the Young and Talented—to do so much damage.

WHY THE NEW BRAND DIDN'T WORK

Wishful thinking. It gets you every time.

The new brand was designed to please its creators: the Brand Experts and the the people at the organization who hired them. As is typical, they were a homogeneous group of youngish, educated, urban professionals with strong opinions about matters of design and communication. They saw anything old-fashioned as toxic: tired, overdone, clichéd.

They despised our direct and literal copy. Our old-line design. Our strong, vivid colors. When the Brand Experts came along and told the organization *Leave all that behind*, it was a dream come true.

What happened was what always happens when you walk away from any established style of communicating: You're also walking away from the audience it was designed for—in this case, the donors who made the organization possible.

Some rebranding efforts never consider the possibility that abandoning your audience might have consequences. They simply walk away from their donors as if there were no such thing as distinct audiences with particular tastes.

The more sophisticated rebrands do it with their eyes open. Our Brand Experts did in-depth research—mainly focus groups—where they discovered an exciting new demographic segment. (I'll describe it later. I bet you can hardly wait to hear about it.) This group promised to be a better fit for the organization than the old donors. They were just waiting to be discovered, like veins of gold under a blighted landscape. They were going to take the organization to new levels because they're wealthier, they care more, and they have the sophistication and education to really appreciate the organization's values and methods. The research reports showed idealized stock-photo images of them: attractive, happy couples who live in gigantic houses.

In real life, our new segment had every desirable characteristic except one: They weren't *donors*.

It doesn't matter how well your brand platform is built if it's designed for people who aren't ready to climb up onto it with you. By the time you realize the painful truth, you've lost most of the people you used to count on to support you year in and year out. Ouch.

It doesn't matter how well your brand platform is built if it's designed for people who aren't ready to climb up onto it with you.

Aiming at unresponsive audiences isn't the only error Brand Experts tend to make.

For the sake of argument, let's imagine that the Brand Experts embraced the donors and understood the fundraising situation clearly—and thus didn't get every single thing wrong. It could happen. I've seen it happen.

Even then, Brand Experts can still create a failure. That's because their work involves more than just ill-considered choices about the audience and communication standards. The commercial-style branding the Brand Experts bring to the table is the *wrong tool* for fundraising. You might as well use a buzz-saw to brush your teeth.

LET'S BE FAIR TO THE BRAND EXPERTS

Am I just a little bit biased against Brand Experts and the work they do with nonprofits? Put it this way: On my list of Undesirable Groups, Brand Experts fall somewhere between Plagues of Locusts and Lobbyists for Puppy Mills.

Now that we've cleared the air about that, I'll be the first to admit that I'm not being completely fair about this. Not all Brand Experts deserve my ire. I'm fully aware I've made the Brand Expert a sort of straw man throughout this book. He's a "poster child" who symbolizes everything that goes awry when nonprofits misapply branding.

But nonprofit branding doesn't always go wrong.

I've met and worked with Brand Experts who get it. They bring branding into organizations in ways that add lasting value. They boost fundraising revenue and tighten the bond with donors. They do exactly what we need them to do.

You could hire Brand Experts and be better for it.

But that's not what this book is about.

We're looking at what can and does go wrong with nonprofit branding, and what you can do instead that will help you accomplish your goals.

So please—be wary, be mindful, be as cagey as a riverboat gambler when it comes to hiring branding help. And here's something that should really make you nervous: You could fend off the bad kind of Brand Experts and still fall victim to the most insidious and dangerous Brand Expert of all: The Brand Expert Within.

Not the turtleneck-clad outsider, but someone inside your organization who longs to solve every problem by applying
(continued)

commercial-style branding to your marketing and fundraising. That person could even be you.

Because there's a little bit of Brand Expert in each of us.

We'd all like to find quick solutions to tough problems like eroding response rates, shrinking market share, and shifting media use. We all feel the weight of the vast budgets of commercial marketing, and we suspect they've discovered secrets we haven't dreamed of. We're all susceptible to the glamour of the advertising world, with its French Riviera award festivals, huge expense accounts, and mind-boggling production budgets. Any of us can walk away from the things we know about donors and how they interact with us, choosing instead empty theories that are so much more exciting.

So when I talk about Brand Experts, I'm not just talking about outsiders. I'm also talking about myself. And I'm talking about you.

HOW COMMERCIAL BRANDING WORKS

Commercial-style branding is a clearly defined discipline, developed over the past hundred years or so for the marketing of goods. To simplify, it takes one of these approaches:

- The old approach: *Buy our stuff because it's great.* (Largely discredited, but still in use.)
- The new, more enlightened approach: *Buy our stuff for your own greatness.*

Both of these approaches generate a series of claims about the benefits of the products they're selling. When done right, these benefits make their claims about greatness believable to their target customers.

In either case, the customer can have a direct experience with the product. If you shell out money for an iPhone, you'll get an iPhone, and you'll quickly know whether it lives up to the promise of the brand. <u>When the brand and product are aligned, it's a successful brand. When the product fails to deliver what the marketing promises, the customer feels cheated.</u>

The whole notion of commercial branding—that you make a promise and fulfill it with a product—*collapses* when you apply it to charitable giving.

Think about what happens when you give money to a charity: If the nonprofit is well run, your donation triggers a prompt, thorough, and specific acknowledgment. If they're really on their game, you'll also get subsequent reports about the impact of your gift. That's nice—and important—but it isn't a firsthand experience.

It's as if you paid for an iPhone and they sent you an envelope full of glowing iPhone product reviews.

You'd be annoyed if Apple did that. But it's not a problem in the world of charitable giving. That's because unlike the experience of buying something, *most of the pleasure you derive from charitable giving happens before you give and while you're giving.* It's the well-documented <u>"warm glow of altruism." It comes from within the donor, not from a direct experience with a product.</u>

This is what evades practitioners of commercial-style branding when they go to work on a nonprofit. In charitable giving, the payment itself is the moment of exchanged value. Paying is not something donors consent to in order to get what they really want. "Paying" is what donors want in the first place.

Commercial branding is not designed to work within this basic reality of charitable giving. That's why it falls so flat when applied to nonprofits.

To see how and where they go astray when they enter the nonprofit world, let's look into the minds of Brand Experts when they're doing their best work. Nike is a brilliant commercial brand. It has managed to make shoes, the most pedestrian of consumer commodities, stand for *human aspiration.*

Footwear designers at Nike might dispute me on this, but let's face it: a shoe is a shoe. A truly great shoe is only slightly better than an okay shoe. Describing the features of a shoe only emphasizes how boring and undifferentiated they really are. It's not effective marketing.

To raise their shoes higher in our minds than pieces of leather you tie to your feet, the Nike branders looked upstream to the *meaning* of the shoe purchase. They asked, "Why do people wear these shoes?" Answer: To help in the pursuit of athletic activities. Then they went farther upstream and asked, "Why do people do these activities?" Answer: Because in one way or another, they're striving for achievement. It could be anything from losing weight to beating a cross-town rival—or a world record. They connected that striving with the striving of famous athletes. Suddenly, a pair of shoes was a glorious thing: *Just Do It.*

In charitable giving, paying is not something donors consent to in order to get what they really want. "Paying" is what donors want in the first place.

That's a well-built commercial brand. It's a triumph of the discipline.

But the same thinking takes you down a different path when you try to apply it to a nonprofit brand. Let's give it a try. . . .

Brand Experts, using the commercial logic they know, assume a donation is just like a purchase. In their world, the purchase is not where the psychological action is. So they pay no attention to the purchase and instead look "upstream" from the purchase to discover what's *really* going on.

They ask a series of questions that are a lot like the Nike shoe questions. Why do people give? To help the poor. Why do they help the poor? To make the world a better place. Within three or four questions, they arrive at what they think is the true purpose of the organization in the deepest sense. Which they assume is also the donor's purpose: the ideal, the deeper meaning. The "Just Do It."

The problem is that the ideal is invariably a lovely abstraction. Instead of providing meals for hungry people, it is a value that's inspiring but vague: *Hope.* An aspiration, not an action.

You might be shocked by how often Brand Experts arrive at Hope. It's almost as if Cap'n Crunch cereal, Ford Motors, and Tiffany Jewelry each independently arrived at *Just Do It* as their brand position.

On the surface, *Hope* looks a lot like *Just Do It*. But it's not even close. It doesn't take a donor anywhere because it doesn't motivate *action*. Abstraction isn't action.

This is the moment when commercial-style branding fails for nonprofits.

The problem compounds and spreads as it seeks ways of expressing itself: It usually finds visual expression in images of proud, happy people. Not people in need, not people donors feel compassion for. Copy has to be vague—not about the realities and concrete actions that change the world, but the high-flown ideals that are supposedly behind the urge to change the world. The brand they build might be stirring and beautiful, but it won't and can't reveal that the charity exists to meet needs, right wrongs, and save the world. This form of branding shows the world as if the desired change had *already happened*.

When you show donors a world where the problem has been solved, you might make them feel good, but you've told them, with absolute clarity, "We don't need you."

This is perhaps the most important point in this book: **Stating abstract ideals is not fundraising.** No matter how elevated those ideals are. Donors give to make specific things happen, not to identify with platonic ideals.

Stating abstract ideals is not fundraising. No matter how elevated those ideals are.

Our job as fundraisers is not to ennoble a boring old shoe with a glowing nimbus of the ideal. Our job is almost the opposite of that: *We connect a donor's ideals with a gritty and specific reality, so she can change the world.*

Commercial-style branding is structurally at odds with that reality.

Nonprofits that have never been through a formal branding process often have stronger brands than those that have.

That's because they haven't wandered into the wilderness of abstract statements about their greatness. Instead, they're presenting their donors with specific actions those donors care about and are willing to pay for.

Even when they aren't savvy or experienced fundraisers, "underbranded" organizations quickly learn by trial and error to be specific and action oriented.

They have little choice but to focus on the real world. They don't have brand guidelines telling them they must rise above that. So they just put out clear, specific fundraising offers that allow donors to do things they want to do. That's how you raise funds. It's not glamorous, and it's not going to win awards or get written up in *Communication Arts*. But it *will* raise money.

Some rare nonprofits don't suffer fundraising disaster, even after they rebrand. They are the ones that already had well-defined fundraising offers that they refuse to abandon:

- They have the calls to action that both donors and people inside the organization understand—and that can't be obliterated by a fog of aspirational abstraction.

- They can make what they do clear and obvious visually and emotionally because they've learned what motivates donors to action.

- They connect with donors. Real donors whose names and preferences they know, not fancy new made-up demographics squeezed out of qualitative research in hopes of finding people they like better.

SUMMARY

If your organization has any visibility at all, the Brand Experts are looking for you. The Color Master, Font Guy, Imagist, Wordsmith, and the small army of suits who corral them see your organization the way a hungry lion sees an overweight, three-legged zebra. They're salivating at the prospect of getting your new brand into their portfolio.

They may charge you a lot or they might do the work for free. Either way, it's going to cost you.

When brand experts come to you offering to build a commercial-style, super-polished, look-at-me brand—*just don't do it!* You can't afford the damage it can do to your relationships with donors and the revenue they provide. Your work is too important.

TAKEAWAYS FOR NONPROFIT BRAND BUILDERS

- Commercial-style branding is almost always the wrong tool for nonprofit organizations. That's why even when it's well executed, it can damage an organization's ability to raise funds.

- Stating abstract ideals is not fundraising. Fundraising is about action—putting specific actions in front of donors so they can change the world in specific ways.

- Creating a brand that's pleasing to you and your colleagues is a costly mistake.

CHAPTER TWO

Branding in the Real World

> Your brand is something your donors experience, not just a
> marketing framework you or your agency dream up. Creating
> that reality for donors is critical. But don't let that keep you
> from building the marketing framework part of your brand.

I'm stuck in a dysfunctional relationship. Abused and unhappy, I
can't break away, even though doing so would take little effort and
improve my life.

Here's the situation: I travel a lot for business, and I fly mostly on
one airline. Let's call it Amalgamated Air.

I appear to be a fanatically loyal customer. Amalgamated probably thinks so. But truth is, there is no corporation in the world I hate
as much as I hate Amalgamated Air.

For decades, Amalgamated Air and its snappish, unhelpful
employees have heaped discomfort, inconvenience, and even physical pain on me. They've kept me up all night, shuffling like a zombie
from one hopeless airport gate to the next. They've lied to my face
about flights that simply weren't coming or going. They've detained
me for pointless hours on overheated airplanes parked on the edges of
airports. They've made me miss important meetings, time with my
family, and whole stretches of my life.

The very mention of the name Amalgamated Air gives me a
gut-wrenching sense of foreboding. I could be relaxing on the
beach, deep in conversation with someone I love, or praying in

church—if I hear the words "Amalgamated Air," I'll instantly become one of those red-faced scowlers you see so often in airports.

If I had a nemesis, a Lex Luthor evil genius obsessed with defeating and tormenting me, I believe he'd fall short of what Amalgamated Air has accomplished.

I'd abandon Amalgamated quicker than you could say "aircraft maintenance," except for the free flights, upgrades, and other privileges my status as a frequent flyer gives me. And, to judge from the tales of other travelers, I could do worse. I'm a classic codependent.

Sooner or later, some smart airline is going to figure out how to provide business travelers like me with the service and reliability we want. Then we'll break free from Amalgamated and its cohorts like inmates scattering through the broken walls of a prison after an earthquake, and we'll run freely over open, fragrant fields. (I can dream, can't I?)

Say what I might about Amalgamated, I have to admit their facilities and airplanes look good. They have an attractive and consistent design scheme that inspires calm and a sense of professionalism. You can recognize it in an instant, no matter what airport you're in. Their marketing looks like their planes and their gates. It captures what you wish travel would be: a magical combination of adventure and connecting with others. They make it seem as if you're always simultaneously setting out on a quest and arriving home from one.

It's a strong, clear, and well-expressed brand. My hat is off to Amalgamated and the Brand Experts who helped them create it.

But almost every time I fly, Amalgamated Air spits on its own brand by delivering experiences that radically contradict the promise the brand makes and the mood it works so hard to cultivate. Day by day, they do more damage to that brand than an army of determined saboteurs or dozens of mocking YouTube videos ever could.

Amalgamated Air is a textbook case of a well-built brand that's plastered over a festering reality. The ideal is dramatically misaligned with the real. It reminds us that your brand is not just *what you say and how you look. It's what you do.* Even more important, *it's what your customers experience.* Your brand is the promise you *keep*, not the one you make.[1]

I bring this up because the sad state of the Amalgamated Air brand can happen to any organization.

THERE IS A BETTER WAY TO BRAND

This book is mostly about the "shallow" part of branding. You could master everything I'm telling you, and still blow it through the heedless actions of employees or partners who don't live your brand.

I really hope you won't do that. It would be a terrible waste of your energy and mine.

To guard against that, I recommend that you read one or more of the many excellent books on the human and cultural side of branding. One of the main things you'll learn from those books is that the deep end of branding is insanely hard to accomplish. Don't think Amalgamated Air is failing at it for lack of trying.

Building the human infrastructure of a great brand will take a long time. It will be painful. You'll have fierce disagreements that could damage relationships. You may have to get rid of people you like—but who can't align with your brand promise. Someone, maybe everyone, will have to disavow treasured beliefs or attitudes. And you'll probably never fully succeed.

Don't let that discourage you. The fact that it's hard—maybe even impossible—to build a deep and foolproof brand from top to bottom should not keep you from improving the visible part now. Don't make perfection the enemy of progress.

There are two reasons you should feel good about "shallow" branding—branding as displayed in marketing—even if you haven't nailed down deep branding:

---

1. Kristin Zhivago, *Rivers of Revenue: What to Do When the Money Stops Flowing* (Jamestown, RI: Smokin' Donut Books, 2004).

1. *"Fake it till you make it" is good advice.* As many religious people know, going through the motions can lead you to the transformation you seek. Most times when I go to church, I don't feel spiritual. I stand, kneel, sing, swallow the bread and the wine—and do it all in a heedless and distracted way. Call me hypocritical—I know I am. Yet somehow, every now and then, I touch the divine; going through the motions of those odd practices somehow lifts me, flinching and unwilling, up to where I wanted to be in the first place.

   Life is like that. It works for organizations as well as people. Acting like you're there helps you get there. Going through the motions of having a brand—doing the things that the great brands do—can help build the brand into the life of your organization.

2. *Even shallow branding will make a positive difference.* Building the visible form of a good brand can quickly improve your revenue. In fact, shallow branding can have more impact on revenue than deep branding does, at least in the short term. There's an 80–20 rule in force here: Just as 80 percent of your revenue comes from 20 percent of your donors, something like 80 percent of the measurable good that can come from a better nonprofit brand comes from the lesser part of the work—the visible part.

   You aren't an airline, where every time something goes awry customers are there to suffer from it. The only experience most of your donors will ever have with you is your fundraising. Even if your staff were packed with donor-hating employees who have toxic interactions with your supporters every single time, most donors will never contact them. They'll never feel the sting of the broken promise.

   Get your fundraising right, and you'll be most of the way to the fine-tuned brand you need.

● ● ●

I doubt there's a nonprofit on this planet with the capacity to inflict its donors as much suffering as an airline, a phone company, or an insurance company. I suppose we should be thankful for that.

When we fail to connect with donors, what happens? They just ignore us. They don't get mad. They don't blog or tweet about our self-centered and irrelevant message. They just ignore us. They don't even realize they're ignoring us.

Badly branded fundraising isn't offensive. (It offends me, and it offends you. But we don't count.) It's not an insult. It doesn't cause discomfort or inconvenience and it doesn't make anyone feel ripped-off or lied to. It's just a zero. It costs us dearly in revenue we never get, but donors will feel no pain. For that reason, they'll never do us the favor of pointing out our failures.

There are some nonprofits that have that kind of impact on their donors. Small, local, specialized organizations, especially houses of worship, have real capacity to make donors unhappy by violating their own brand. (You haven't seen fury until you've seen the fury of someone who feels betrayed by his church.)

But every nonprofit should pay attention to failing and broken commercial brands—how they turn once-proud businesses into a sad drag on the economy and on society. Put them in your rearview mirror and make as much progress as you can. Starting with the outward form of your brand.

You don't have to follow the path of Amalgamated Air and others like them.

CHAPTER THREE

What Branding Work Can Do to Fundraising Revenue

> Most typical branding activities have predictable impacts on fundraising revenue. The news is not good: Most of these activities are likely to be harmful.

Those direct-response ads in comic books beguiled my brother and me: Sea monkeys! X-ray specs! A *real submarine!* But the prices were always just out of reach.

One ad finally snared us: The headline shouted: "100 PC. TOY SOLDIER SET." The illustration showed lines of soldiers among tanks and cannons, all shooting at unseen enemies. Airplanes roared overhead. A flotilla of ships steamed across a distant sea. There was a list of all 100 pieces: a treasure trove of fighting men and their materiel.

The clincher, oddly, was a subhead: *Packed in this pasteboard footlocker.* There was an arrow pointing at what looked like a military footlocker. We didn't know what pasteboard was, but it sounded sturdy, and the footlocker alone seemed worth the $1.25, shipping included. So we pooled our quarters and sent them off with the coupon.

Six to eight weeks later, the footlocker appeared in the mailbox. The fact that it fit in the mailbox, nestled between envelopes, was the first sign something wasn't quite right. It was about the size of those boxes the bank mails your blank checks in. And pasteboard, it turned out, was a flimsy version of cardboard.

If you ordered this set of toy soldiers from a comic book, you got exactly what the ad promised. That was the problem.

The reason a hundred soldiers and military vehicles fit in such a small box was this: They were flat—like bas-relief sculptures. And small. The soldiers were about half the height of standard toy soldiers. Worse yet, the tanks, airplanes, battleships were even smaller, not in scale with the men who supposedly operated them. It was as if the toy soldiers had their own toy trucks, tanks, ships, and airplanes. Everything was made of a sharp-edged, brittle plastic. Many of the soldiers couldn't stand up because the plastic bases at their feet were bent. In my memory, they even smelled bad.

We half-heartedly set up those pieces that could stand and enacted a small, indecisive battle. Then we packed it all back into the pasteboard footlocker and put it away. We fumed for a while about reporting the company to The Authorities, but we knew our threats were empty: Even though the set was a cruel travesty for boys who liked to play with soldiers, they'd delivered exactly what the ad promised. After that, every time we saw that little box, we felt a pang of regret. We'd been had.

A lot of kids who grew up in the 1950s, 1960s, and 1970s had experiences like ours. That was how it went with the stuff offered in comic book ads. Don't get me started about sea monkeys. Learning to be skeptical about marketing is part of growing up in America.

Skepticism would also serve nonprofits when they consider the services of Brand Experts. Their offerings are not unlike those in the comic book advertisements: They deliver *exactly what they promise*: a set of attractive, colorful documents on slick paper, detailing everything they said they'd detail. It's all there . . . but the new brand is a big disappointment.

Revenue is far more likely to go down than up when you get your new brand. Those new, richer, more involved donors fail to swarm in. Meanwhile, the old donors go into accelerated attrition—because they no longer recognize you, their old friend. The entire fundraising program spirals painfully downward. You'd be far better off with a box of bas-relief toy soldiers.

I know this because I've had front-row seats at dozens of nonprofit rebrandings. I've heard the promises, watched the buildup of anticipation—then felt the cold splash of reality that followed the roll-out of the new brand.

Not always. But it goes that way so often, it's the normal experience nonprofits have with Brand Experts.

Please don't take this as a warning against *all* branding activity. Not everything brand-related is harmful. If you do it right, you can boost fundraising. It could even change the game for your organization.

So how do you tell the difference between branding that solves a problem and branding that makes you wish you'd chosen a different profession?

You need what I needed when I was a kid: an older cousin who'd ordered all the comic-book junk and could report what each of those temptations was like in real life. You're in luck. I'll be your cousin for the next few pages. I'll show you in gory detail what to expect financially when you put the most common rebranding practices to work.

What you're about to read is controversial. If they read this book (and I doubt they will), Brand Experts and people who believe in them will protest that these conclusions are out of context or too broad. But these figures come from years of firsthand observations. They have been remarkably consistent.

I can't guarantee your experiences will be the same as mine. But hold on to your hat, because you may be in for a shock or two when you see the impact of what you may have considered smart changes.

IF YOU CHANGE YOUR LOGO

Impact on revenue: None.

No kidding. Change your logo and revenue stays where it is. (That's as long as there isn't also a name change and/or cause-identification change. I'll tell you about that shortly.)

This might surprise you. It knocked my socks off the first time I saw it. (I thought a logo change was going to deep-six my client. It didn't.)

Typically, a lot of hope and anxiety surround a logo change. Some people say the old logo is dated, poorly connected to the cause, or just bad. They believe the new logo will be a ray of light that will finally illuminate the cause and encourage new levels of generosity. Others are afraid the change will leave donors confused and unsure of their identity, leading to a drop in giving.

Then the new logo rolls out. Nothing happens. Nothing good, nothing bad.

I've seen clunky old legacy logos replaced with much better ones—and the revenue needle didn't even wobble. I've also seen decent old logos we thought had brand equity replaced with goofy abstractions that should have killed us—and we didn't even sustain a flesh wound.

Does your logo even matter?

Of course it does. A logo helps signify that an organization is "real." It acts as a sort of anchor that holds you in a donor's mind, the way stained glass windows tell you you're in a church, or a certain shape of hat tells you someone is a police officer. A logo does this important job whether it's good or bad.

As we'll see shortly, colors and shapes don't have much horsepower in fundraising. Images have enormous power to inform and inspire (as we'll see later)—but that power resides mostly in photographs, not in logos.

And I hate to break it to you, but your logo is not as famous as you might think it is. Few nonprofit logos are. What's the chance your donors will be confused by a new logo if they can't recall the old one? Anyway, they aren't going to be inspired to new levels of altruism by a logo they don't quite notice.

Some nonprofit logos matter a lot: I'm guessing that if The Salvation Army (Exhibit 3.1) traded in its venerable red-shield logo, things might not turn out as revenue neutral. But then, the Army's recognizability rivals the logo of Coca-Cola and other commercial super-brands.

IF YOU CHANGE YOUR GRAPHIC STANDARDS

Impact on revenue: Negative, but small.

I'm not referring to the changes in look that happen over time as designers come and go and as styles shift. I mean the mandated (and usually extensive) design standards you find in graphics standards manuals produced by Brand Experts.

Graphic standards are meant to "protect the brand" by putting strict and detailed controls on font, color palette, photo treatment, and other aspects of design. It's the work Brand Experts are most proud of—their Sistine Chapel. But when it

EXHIBIT 3.1

The Salvation Army's logo is probably the most recognized nonprofit logo of all time, and among the top logos across all categories. Most nonprofit logos have zero mindshare by comparison.

comes to motivating donor behavior, these graphic standards books don't make a big difference.

Why? Seasoned direct-response pros will tell you that design is not where the leverage is. *What you say* matters more than *how you look while saying it.* That wonderful new font that captures the essence of your cause? It has almost no impact. Those exciting new colors and ingenious design rules that speak your dreams? They might as well be trees falling in the forest with no one to hear them.

Seasoned direct-response pros will tell you that design is not where the leverage is. What you say *matters much more than* how you look while saying it.

When design has any impact at all, it's usually to depress revenue. That's because so often the new standards move away from bold colors, classic fonts designed for readability, and the out-of-date look that appeals to older donors. The official look is less readable, less likable, and less persuasive. Fortunately, the negative impact is slight.

My guess (and I have to guess because I haven't seen it happen) is that if a change in graphic standards were toward better readability, more emotion, and audience appropriateness, there'd be a small *positive* impact on fundraising revenue.

IF YOU CHANGE YOUR COPY STANDARDS

Impact on revenue: Usually negative, but small; potentially worse.

Only the most ambitious rebrands put as much focus on copy as they do on design. Face it, fellow copywriters: Words are tedious. Most Brand Experts don't care enough about copy to mess around with it. *Thank goodness for that!* If Brand Experts sunk their claws into copy as deeply as they do to design, the loss in revenue might be steep.

I've heard Brand Experts and their disciples speak out against foundational fundraising copy approaches. Things like:

- Directly addressing the donor, because doing so "lacks the professional dignity of the brand."

- Openly mentioning money, "because we're about hope, not cash."

- Employing a sense of urgency, because "it's phony."

Fortunately, these delusional proclamations seldom get codified into brand guidelines.

Brand copy guidelines tend to be few and cosmetic, with a nit-picky focus on political correctness and schoolmarm grammar rules. (Speaking as a former English teacher, I'm amazed how often these grammar and usage rules are flat-out incorrect, in addition to being bad for fundraising.)

My experience is that over time, enforcement of copy guidelines gets more and more lax. That's right: Copy is so boring for Brand

Experts they can't bring themselves to focus on it enough to ruin it. This is something to be thankful for.

IF YOU CHANGE YOUR ORGANIZATION'S NAME

Impact on revenue: 25 to 50 percent loss.

Yes, you read that right. Changing your name could wallop your fundraising. I'm sorry to report that the revenue drops have been that bad every time I've seen a branding-motivated name change.[1]

An organization's name, unlike its logo, appears to be a piece of real estate your donors know. When a name changes, a meaningfully large segment of donors lose track of the organization. Or maybe the change arouses distrust. Whatever it is, campaigns underperform and donor retention falls after a name change.

WHAT'S UP WITH THESE LEGENDARY NAMES?

Some top-brand nonprofits have names that don't reveal what they do: The Salvation Army, United Way, and Red Cross, to name three gold-plated brands.

You might draw the conclusion that an opaque, nonliteral name is an important brand asset. That's what some Brand Experts seem to believe.

The Brand Experts are missing something important. It's as if they're standing in a parking lot next to the Grand Canyon and concluding that the excellent pavement of the lot is what attracts so many cars to this remote spot.

(continued)

---

1. I should point out one exception I know about: In Australia, the Spastics Centre rebranded as the Cerebral Palsy Alliance, and has continued to grow since.

What these organizations have that the rest of us don't have is not just brand equity, but generations of up-close, high-quality brand equity. They've been around forever, patiently excelling at what they do, and doing it somewhere near virtually everyone. That's why everyone knows what they do. (At least everyone *thinks* they know what they do.)

Time, omnipresence, and a good record give these top nonprofit brands a kind of superpower that's far beyond whatever their name accomplishes on its own. They've made their names great, not vice versa.

Unless your Brand Experts can travel through time, they can't cook up that kind of brand equity, no matter how smart they are.

The rest of us johnnies-come-lately without time machines have to be more literal. Our names should make it completely clear what we do—or better yet, what the donor can do. We'll be best off with names like these:

- American Cancer Society (along with the host of disease-focused charities with literal names)
- Food for the Poor
- Make-a-Wish Foundation
- Save the Children
- World Wildlife Foundation
- Wounded Warrior Project

This isn't the only approach to nonprofit names. But it's probably the best if you're trying to get traction among donors.

The most revenue-crushing name changes are those that make it *less clear what the organization does*. And that's exactly what Brand Experts often want to do with your brand: free it from mundane literalism and launch it skyward with unspecific (thus unlimited) aspirations. Sounds beautiful. But it's a costly mistake.

The name changes on the less harmful end of the spectrum are smaller shifts that preserve something of the old name. If "Help the Hungry Seattle" becomes "Help the Hungry Puget Sound," less harm would be done than if they dubbed themselves "NutriCityNW." (Made-up words are the worst possible form of name change. Trust me.)

The sobering thing about nonprofit name changes is that you can expect to take a hit even if the change is an *improvement*. Suppose the old name was eccentric and the new name is literal: the change probably hurts. This is just one of those cases where we can accurately say *change is (mostly) bad*.

There's a thin silver lining around this dark cloud: The revenue loss after a name change is probably temporary. You won't like my definition of *temporary*. It can take three or more years for donor revenue to claw its way back to where it was before the change.

IF YOU MUST CHANGE YOUR NAME

Reasons for changing your name:

- Your geographic service area has changed (grown, shrunk shifted) so the name is now inaccurate.
- The mission has changed so much that the name is no longer accurate.
- There's been a scandal that causes many to distrust you.

If you must change your name, make the change as minor and insignificant as possible:

- The Atlanta Homeless Coalition might become the Greater Atlanta Homeless Coalition.

(continued)

- Pug Rescue might become Pug and Pals Rescue.
- Missoula Opera might become Missoula Opera and Ballet.

If there's no way to make your name change incremental, here's a workaround that may save your bacon: *Use both names together for a period.* This allows supporters to keep track of who you are while the new name to get its foothold. This can help you avoid the revenue loss a cold-turkey change would bring. This two-name period should last at least a year—probably longer.

IF YOU CHANGE YOUR CAUSE IDENTIFICATION

Impact on revenue: 20 to 30 percent loss.

Sometimes Brand Experts dream up an exciting new way to describe what an organization does—a perfect little koan that crystallizes the cause in a whole new way. That might sound like a great idea. But you'll really wish they hadn't.

Your cause identification is the basic description of what you do. The type of change I'm talking about is where an organization does something like this:

- An organization that used to "feed the hungry" becomes, after the Brand Experts' magic is applied, "a champion of wholeness for the new century." (Don't laugh—I'm not exaggerating!)
- An organization that used to say it "helps the homeless" now "brings hope to the inner city."
- A "Cancer Center" becomes a "Health Center."

You may have noticed something about these examples. Each change makes the description *more abstract.* That's what Brand Experts tend to do. That's why it usually hurts revenue.

A change in cause identification can happen with or without a name change. The Smith County Land Conservancy might wisely realize that there is equity in their name. But, weary of same-oldness, they might stop talking about saving land from harmful development and replace that cause identification with a vague statement about creating memories for the future.

When they do that, they'll leave donors confused and disconnected, even though they kept their name. We can only hope that Smith County conservation donors will remember—or eventually rediscover—what the organization has done all along.

WHEN NONPROFITS DENY THEIR MISSION

Over the years, I've collected dozens of goofy proclamations by nonprofit organizations that publicly denied that they did what they did.

These were not shady organizations. Not one had anything to be ashamed of. And none of them had actually changed their mission. But they categorically repudiated the very things their name, mission statement, or marketing said they did.

It's as if an organization called Save the Trees announced, "We don't save trees."

You might think they lost their marbles.

That's not exactly what happened. They saw their denials as visionary attempts to be more compelling or accurate. When Save the Trees says, "We don't save trees," they mean one of two things:

- "We don't *only* save trees. We do a lot of other cool things, too."
- "Our method for saving trees is so complex that 'save the trees' seems like a mere caricature of what we do."

Either one of those might be true. But both are terrible reasons for denying what you clearly are.

(continued)

The people at Save the Trees may think "We don't save trees" is an elegant rhetorical device that will spark interest and inspire donors to higher levels of understanding and support.

To your donors, it's more like a slap across the face with a wet kipper. They're the people you've succeeded in bringing on board. They've bought in to the mission. They *care* about saving the trees!

Count on this: Your donors have a less sophisticated view of your mission than you do. They don't spend 40 hours a week, year in and year out, thinking about it. It doesn't bore them. It doesn't seem oversimplified. Your cause is compelling and worthwhile to your donors. Otherwise, they wouldn't be giving.

Unless you've truly abandoned your core mission, acting like you have is confusing at best, and self-destructive at worst.

Don't do it.

There are reasons for changing a cause identification. If Save the Stoats used to say they work to protect endangered stoats—but now they also work with threatened weasels, they shouldn't change their cause identification to an abstract, poetic phrase that vaguely covers what they do to help stoats and their cousins. They should keep on saying they protect stoats. And sometimes add that they protect weasels, too.

● ● ●

These aren't predictions of what *will happen* with your rebranding; they are what I've seen happen in real life. Repeatedly. The damage is only potential, but it's potential in the way a grand piano falling off a skyscraper has the potential to make a lot of noise.

You're an alert reader, so you've probably have noticed a striking feature of these brand changes: The *best* outcome I've seen from all these branding activities is *revenue neutral*.

Organizations have gone through all the pain, anxiety, and expense to improve their brand, and in the best cases, there was no impact. More often, something terrible happened.

The few times I've observed a re-brand that *wasn't* followed by a revenue drop, I popped the champagne cork. A harmless rebranding? It's a miracle! It's as if there'd been a flaming, 50-car pile-up on the freeway, and nobody died.

That's a *low bar for success*—wouldn't you say? Given that the whole point of changing an organization's brand is to *improve revenue*, I have to conclude the obvious: *Corporate-style branding is bad for nonprofits.*

That doesn't mean all branding work is bad for nonprofits. Being against branding is like being against oxygen. Brand is all around us, all the time, impossible to avoid. Like it or not, you can't escape it. You'd wither away if you somehow could separate yourself from brand.

If something about your brand is broken—confusing, messy, self-contradicting—I hope you'll take steps to fix it.

Being against branding is like being against oxygen. Brand is all around us, all the time, impossible to avoid.

In the next few chapters, we'll move away from the *don'ts* of branding and look at branding activities that can *enhance your fundraising*.

I'll show you some alternative branding activities most Brand Experts don't know about. Once you know these things, you won't be tempted by the branding offers that are most likely turn out to be so painful and disappointing.

The services of Brand Experts have a lot in common with those comic book ads, like sea monkeys (they aren't grinning aquatic humanoids, but white specks that move aimlessly about in their water for a few weeks), X-ray specs (you can't see through clothing or anything else), and the *real submarine* (it's just a cardboard box you sit in; if you took to the sea in it, you'd drown). They promise such greatness but deliver such pain.

Save your money for something better.

TAKEAWAYS FOR NONPROFIT BRAND BUILDERS

- Feel free to change your logo. Doing so is unlikely to hurt you, and you may end up with something better.

- Change (or codify) your graphic standards, but do so with caution and a light hand. Be sure you are making your look more appropriate to your donors, not less (and make sure it's your real donors, not some new group the Brand Experts say they'll discover). Aim for readability and simplicity. An up-to-the-minute modern look is probably not appropriate.

- Draw up copy guidelines, but don't overdo it. Avoid political correctness, formal usage rules, and your boss's pet peeves. Make your guidelines focus on creating messages that are clear, simple, and persuasive.

- Avoid changing your name—unless external changes make it unavoidable. If you must, make the change as incremental as possible. Remember, this is likely to be the most costly change of all.

- Don't change your cause identification. If your mission has "evolved," communicate what's new and better about it through your messaging and your calls to action. Not through wholesale denial of the cause your donors support.

CHAPTER FOUR

We're Being Brandjacked

A Guide to Survival

> It's not always easy to tell useful branding work from the type
> that will scuttle your revenue. This chapter shows you some of
> the key warning signs.

Remember the tale of the hapless business traveler who had a drink
with an attractive stranger in a hotel bar? He woke up the next
morning in a bathtub of ice water and a note saying one of his
kidneys had been "harvested."

When that urban legend made the rounds, I knew a guy who
believed it. Really believed it. He was a frequent traveler and an
extrovert who enjoyed conversations with strangers—"new
friends," he called them. The story seemed completely plausible
to him, which made it completely terrifying.

This guy didn't just let his fear fester. He drew up a list of
warning signs: signals that the new friend you've just met might
have her eyes on one of your kidneys. He e-mailed his list around to
other business travelers, and that's when I read it. I remember only
one of the warning signs: "She asks a lot of questions about your
health."

Don't worry—you don't really need the rest of the list. You aren't
likely to have your kidneys harvested against your will.

But there's a different danger you should guard against: If you
work at a nonprofit, there's a good chance there's a Brand Expert

who has your organization in her sights, plotting a sly attack that could leave you figuratively wounded and gasping in a bathtub full of icy water.

I call it *brandjacking*—when Brand Experts remake a nonprofit brand and render it ineffective for fundraising.

Not all branding work is brandjacking. No more than everyone you meet is out to purloin your internal organs. You might need expert help clarifying your messaging, reining in design anarchy, or improving the connection between what your organization does and what you say about it in public. These are useful services that can do your organization a lot of good. If you need these things, I hope you get them.

Brandjacking: *When Brand Experts remake a nonprofit brand and render it ineffective for fundraising.*

Brandjacking is a different thing. It's a radical restructuring of your public face, *based on the logic of commercial branding.* It's done with little knowledge about fundraising or understanding of donors. In Chapter 3, you saw what some of the common misapplied branding activities can cost. But it's hard to discern the difference between legitimate marketing help and brandjacking.

The insidious thing about brandjacking is that it requires cooperation from the victim. If it happens to you, you'll be fully conscious from the first thrilling briefing to the last round of layoffs. You might be confused or bamboozled, but you'll be as awake as you are right now.

Furthermore, brandjackers look no different from regular people. (They usually dress nicer, but that's hardly enough to go on.)

That's why I've drawn up a list of warning signs to help you cut through the confusion and detect a brandjacking before things go too far.

THE SIX WARNING SIGNS OF A BRANDJACKING

1. The new brand is not aimed at your donors.
2. The new brand requires you to abandon your donors.
3. The branding work is not grounded in donor behavior.
4. The new brand describes your cause in a symbolic way.
5. The new brand requires absolute consistency.
6. The new brand is design and little else.

BRANDJACKING WARNING SIGN 1: THE NEW BRAND IS NOT AIMED AT YOUR DONORS

Consultants like to make their clients happy. Believe me, it's more enjoyable to hear clients say they love what you've done than "It's so . . . corny" or "The chairman of the board hates it. Change everything."

Aiming your message at *donors* causes these awkward moments. When you aim at donors, you often miss nonprofit staff.

That's where Brand Experts have a tactical advantage over fundraising specialists. They can aim their messaging and design squarely at nonprofit staff. They can create happiness and pride throughout your organization. They can make you feel, perhaps for the first time in your career, that an outside consultant *gets you*. Unlike those fundraising people, who kept creating messages that are so brash, simplistic, and old-fashioned—that is, aimed at donors.

Brandjackers take care to stay away from measurable financial impact. That's how they aim the brand at *you* and make you happy. They don't have to reach out to those pesky donors.

It's not a plot to defraud you. Few Brand Experts have any idea they're doing it. Most of them never quite grasp the troublesome fact that *you and your donors are not the same people.* That you belong to different demographic groups, have different tastes, different expectations—and these differences mean *what works for you will not motivate donors.* And vice versa.

■ 43 ■

Without that key piece of intelligence, Brand Experts can sail through the whole branding process unconscious of the fact that making the brand pleasing to you means they are destroying your fundraising.

One of the most important secrets to success in fundraising: Effective fundraising always makes you at least slightly uncomfortable.

If you promise not to tell my competitors, I'll give you one of the most important and little-known secrets to success in fundraising: *Effective fundraising always makes you at least slightly uncomfortable.* It's a bit like seeing your parents making out. You know it's a good thing, but it's not something you care to dwell on. You're the wrong audience.

Many people working at nonprofits spend all their time in that mom-and-dad-making-out state of discomfort with the work. But they don't realize the discomfort is *normal.* Unavoidable. They never make peace with it, because they think their discomfort is a sign there's something wrong with their fundraising. Actually, it's a clear sign that there's something right with it.

That's why lack of discomfort is a warning sign. If brand work makes you and other insiders happy, proud, and comfortable, it's likely a brandjacking. It's designed to tickle *your* fancy. But it's liable to sink your fundraising effectiveness.

BRANDJACKING WARNING SIGN 2: THE NEW BRAND REQUIRES YOU TO ABANDON YOUR DONORS

Even if your brand is a haphazard Frankenstein's monster without a coherent focus, it has probably been influenced by your donors. They've shaped the message through their responses in measurable direct-response channels. If you clean up the "mess," you may leave behind the donors who helped you make that mess valuable and functional.

If you understand that, you should be brandjacking-proof. Sadly, some nonprofit staffs are so hungry for an all-new, more-pleasing brand, they're willing to adapt a wild and exciting proposal from the Brand Experts: *Get rid of your donors*—those tiresome people who stubbornly respond to the old marketing we dislike. *Replace those donors with different donors,* they say. Better donors who will *get it*.

If you've been in any kind of marketing long enough to have a few gray hairs, you can probably predict what happens when an organization walks away from its supporters. If you haven't, listen to the sad story of the Cynical Humanitarians.

A nonprofit I worked with hired some Brand Experts and told them, "Our fundraising works, but we hate it. It's tacky. We're embarrassed to show it to our friends. Please give us a brand that we'll love—and that still raises the funds we need."

The Brand Experts knew exactly what to say: "It's not your fault; it's the donors. They're too old. Too uneducated. Too down-market. We'll do the research and find a demographic segment you deserve. They'll respond to marketing you'll feel good about."

They came back three months later with an impressive volume of research. They'd discovered a slice of the Great American Pie that they called "Cynical Humanitarians."

I was at the meeting where the Brand Experts presented their findings. The Cynical Humanitarians were urban, educated professionals, younger than traditional donors, well traveled, and not likely to respond to traditional fundraising methods or media. ("They're too smart for direct mail," the report noted.) There were tens of millions of them, clustered in the cities and on the coasts. They were frequently missed by traditional fundraising, because it triggered their well-developed cynicism.

They didn't show up on anybody's fundraising radar because they didn't give to charity in meaningful numbers. They weren't on rental lists, and they didn't spend time on nonprofit web sites. Those things didn't reach them. They were simply waiting for a new type of fundraising to unlock their generosity, the Brand Experts explained. We were going to be there *first*.

I'm used to thinking about donors in an almost anthropological way. Maybe you know what I mean. It's as if we quietly visit their community and take notes, searching for patterns and truth. This wasn't like that. As the Brand Experts described the reading and entertainment habits of the Cynical Humanitarians, I got the strangest feeling: *They were describing me!* I read those magazines! I listen to NPR! I feel that way about politicians! Just like the Cynical Humanitarians, I want to make the world a better place but suspect that many attempts to make things better don't really work. I ignore advertising because I think it's either irrelevant, stupid, or a pack of lies!

The Brand Experts were describing not only me, but most of the people in the room. Who knew? We were all Cynical Humanitarians.

It was an exhilarating feeling: Donors we understood. Donors who would not present us with inexplicable tastes or unfathomable attitudes. Donors whose thoughts we could divine—because their thoughts were our thoughts. We *knew our donors.*

Of course, it would take radically different messaging and whole new channels to reach the Cynical Humanitarians. And our new approaches and channels would never reach or persuade our current donors and prospects. But that was exactly the genius of it. Out with the old! In with the new!

Fast-forward a few months.

Everything we did to reach the Cynical Humanitarians failed— all the Brand Experts' recommendations, as well as many other attempts we cooked up to try and rescue the project. Not a single project came even close to working.

Everything. Failed.

When things go wrong in fundraising, they usually go *slightly* wrong. Response dips by 10 percent. Average gift slides a couple of dollars. Not here. This was dramatic, record-breaking failure. Several of my own personal worsts happened during the Cynical Humanitarian campaigns.

In the end, we'd netted ourselves about 100 Cynical Humanitarian donors—at a net loss of thousands of dollars per donor. To put that in perspective, in a normal year, we brought in several tens of thousands of new donors at a small net cost each. If that weren't bad

THE RIGHT WAY TO EXPAND YOUR DONOR BASE

Abandoning your donors in in order to replace them with a whole crop of new-and-improved donors is a big mistake. *Expanding* the population you can raise funds from is smart.

The way to do that is to take your message to people who are "next door" to your current donors in some way.

- If your donors are ages 65 and up (which most likely they are), seek new donors ages 55 to 65—people who are approaching the donor phase of life. Get there early, and you could have some great donors who support you for a long time.

- If you're doing well in Wisconsin, expand into Minnesota.

- If you've got the Presbyterian market all sewn up, try going to Lutherans.

- You've heard that "birds of a feather flock together." It's also true of certain mammals, such as donors. Your donors have like-minded neighbors. Try campaigns that target zip codes where you already have concentrations of donors.

enough, we eventually found that 85 percent of these new donors never gave another gift. Their retention was less than a third of that of our old donors.

Apparently, the Cynical Humanitarians were too cynical to be donors. More to the point, they were too young. They had all the hallmarks of people their age: unresponsive to fundraising, even messages tailored to them and presented in their preferred channels, and far less likely than traditional donors to stick around and give again.

We switched back to our old-faithful donors, the ones who responded to the fundraising nobody liked.

The cost of the whole Cynical Humanitarian experiment was millions of dollars, considering the value of the donors we didn't get while we were chasing the dream demographic.

There's a diabolic cleverness to the all-new-donors ploy. It feels so right. So exciting. In theory, it *could* work. But the chance of success is microscopic, and the consequence of failure is devastating.

BRANDJACKING WARNING SIGN 3: THE WORK IS NOT GROUNDED IN DONOR BEHAVIOR

One of the great blessings of fundraising is that we're forced to use direct-response marketing in order to gather donations. When we get it right, more donors give, give more, or give more often. When we get it wrong, those numbers drop. We can quickly correct whatever we're doing wrong.

There's no way we can fake it with relativistic advertising metrics like "noted," "awareness," or "impressions." We live or die by numbers you can take to the bank.

This makes us hypersensitive to donors—who they are, what they think, what motivates them. Not what we *wish*. Not what research subjects claim when asked. Only donors' *actual behavior* matters to us.

Sometimes, Brand Experts do research on donors. But it's almost always qualitative research—mainly focus groups and surveys—that give a lot of information about what people are willing to say out loud, but almost no hints about what they *do*.

> *There's one way to know if your cool new idea is going to work: test your ideas in direct-response media before you roll it out.*

There's one way to know if your cool new idea is going to work: test your ideas in direct-response media before you roll it out. This would have saved many organizations from the horrific financial tailspin that ill-conceived branding inflicted on them. If your Brand Experts propose direct-response testing, that's an indication their work is *not* a brandjacking.

Otherwise, stop the press the moment they pooh-pooh testing.

How does a small organization test?

THINGS I'VE LEARNED IN FOCUS GROUPS

I love focus groups: The camaraderie in that darkened room behind the one-way glass. The stories we invent about the participants. The snacks.

I always wait for someone to say *more bang for my buck* about why they choose one charity over another. And it always happens. The phrase ricochets around the room. They all want more bang for their buck.

That's a useful piece of information. It means the concept of *more bang for my buck,* maybe even that exact phrase, potentially has motivational power in fundraising.

I say *potentially* because it's only a hypothesis until you observe it in actual donor behavior.

And that's the main thing we need to know about focus groups: There's a canyon-sized chasm between what people *say* in focus groups and what they *do* in the privacy of their homes.

When you ask the people in a focus group their opinion, a lot of social calculations go into their answers. They may be concerned about what their opinions signal about them to others in the group. They want to be well thought of. They may be angling for a position within the group—leader, influencer, rebel.

There's one thing about focus groups that's even more predictable than the "bang for my buck" comment: If you show them anything that's at all like your successful fundraising materials, they *hate* it. They gang up on it and excoriate everything about it. There's even a facial expression many focus group participants make when they see your best material: the "success sneer."

Send that same material as an e-mail or direct-mail piece, and it's a big winner. That's because in those real-life contexts, people attend to your message without social considerations. They'll either understand and be motivated to give—or not.

(continued)

Social questions like *Will that lady across the table think I'm shallow if I like this?* don't come up.

~~Focus groups are more accurate at counterpredicting success in fundraising than they are at predicting it,~~ If you know that, it can be part of the fun.

If you don't know that, your focus groups are likely to lead you to some expensive surprises.

BRANDJACKING WARNING SIGN 4: THE NEW BRAND DESCRIBES YOUR CAUSE IN A SYMBOLIC WAY

I did well in school because I have a talent for symbolic reasoning. I can write and talk with ease about the hidden meaning and symbolism of just about anything. You may have this talent, too. So do most Brand Experts. All of us belong to a tribe of symbolic thinkers. We make our humanities professors happy, and most of us choose careers in communications.

Over time, we form the illusion that *everyone* thinks in symbols, metaphors, and hidden messages. That's because most of our friends and colleagues think that way. When we hang out together, we entertain ourselves with wordplay, clever allusions, puns, and other forms of symbolic reasoning. It's a way of thinking and communicating that makes us feel comfortable and clever.

But, really, we symbolic thinkers are rare outside of humanities departments. Most people have no gift for symbolic reasoning—and no interest in fostering it. Puzzling out the hidden meaning of a clever metaphor isn't a fun challenge—it's annoying and frustrating. It's about as entertaining for them as searching for misplaced car keys.

A talent for symbolic reasoning is of little use once you leave school. It's even less useful in fundraising. In fact, it can lead you disastrously astray. You might as well raise funds using Cockney Rhyming Slang as rely on symbolism to motivate donors.

SILLY SYMBOLISM IN NONPROFIT MARKETING

Brand Experts sometimes create visual metaphors to symbol-ize what nonprofits do. They'll tell you that describing causes in a literal way is too boring to capture people's attention.

They're terribly wrong about that. Being literal and specific is the *only* dependable way to raise funds.

The lengths to which Brand Experts go to avoid being literal can be funny. Here are a few of my favorite forays into the world of nonprofit abstract symbolism:

- A gun made out of balloons—the long, thin kind clowns twist into whimsical little dachshunds—stands for the problem of child soldiers. The text: *It's easy to convince children that killing is a game.*

- Next to an older man's head, a warning dialog box of the kind served up by the Windows operating system. It tells us that the hard drive "Roger" has "0 Bytes of Disk Space, and contains 0 files, 0 Documents." Yes, someone thinks that is a compelling way to talk about Alzheimer's disease.

- We see the top of a pen, heavily damaged. It's been chewed up. The text says, *Some countries treat journalists the way you treat a pen.* This is considered a crystal-clear way to depict the problem of the repression of journalists.

- Warplanes from around the world converge on Myanmar and drop *flowers* onto a strangely human-devoid land-scape. It's supposed to make us care more about the human rights situation there. That's right: human rights with no humans.

These mind games are a clear sign of brandjacking, or perhaps an ad agency trying to create work that can win awards. (Adver-tising industry awards judges *love* clever visual metaphors.)

To see these ads and many more like them, visit my blog at www.futurefundraisingnow.com and look for "Stupid Nonprofit Ads."

Most Brand Experts, however, rely heavily on symbolism. When *helping the poor* is abandoned as a description of the cause and replaced with something like *sharing hope*, you probably have a brandjacking in progress.

I bring up *hope* (again) because it often shows up during a brandjacking. Think about it: Feeding the hungry generates hope. So does curing a disease. And improving a community. Any time you solve a problem, make people's lives better, or in any way make the world safer, fairer, cleaner, or more beautiful—you can be said to increase *hope.*

Hope may be the thing with feathers that perches in the soul and sings, but it's not a platform for successful fundraising. It's far too general by itself to make donors' hearts swell with compassion.

Donors give to accomplish specific actions, not to solve mental puzzles.

Donors give to accomplish specific actions, not to solve mental puzzles. Brandjackers will usually tell you otherwise as they create their inspiring mental abstractions.

BRANDJACKING WARNING SIGN 5: THE NEW BRAND REQUIRES ABSOLUTE CONSISTENCY

Most brand standards manuals have a section that shows the many ways you *must not use the logo*. It's a funny mixture of things no sane designer would ever do (like distort the logo into a trapezoid) and things that you can hardly avoid doing in real life (like put other things near the logo).

When I look at that section, I enjoy playing out in my mind what drove the Brand Experts to the examples they chose. Did they once have an intern who thought a mirror-image logo would be a good idea? And where did they pick up the belief that type encroaching within an en space of the logo will cause it to shrivel into an unrecognizable lump of bad marketing?

Truth is, minor transgressions of their design ultra-orthodoxy won't hurt a thing. And frankly, though I'd never recommend it, even crazy distortions of the logo are unlikely to have any measurable impact on revenue—as we saw in Chapter 3.

Consistency is good. But it's not always the right thing for effective fundraising. In fact, variety is one of the most dependable fundraising "techniques" at your disposal. If you always do something a certain way—say, you mail your appeal letters in blue envelopes—change that. Try a white envelope. You will likely see an increase in response.

Variety, even fairly meaningless variety, is good at shaking loose extra response. Meaningful variety is even more important. Good fundraising is a relationship. It goes through seasons. It responds to events. That means sometimes you need to shout or cry, to laugh or mourn. When you adhere to an unchanging standard, you can't effectively do that.

If the boy who cried wolf had been smarter (and less deceptive), he might have most days cried "All is well!" Then when the wolf showed up, his cry of "Wolf!" would have gotten a great click-through rate. If he'd had Brand Experts helping him, he would have been consistent, crying "Hope!" in the approved font every day. Including that terrible day when the wolf finally came. That's no different from crying "Wolf" every day. It's just as false, and ends up with the same unpleasant outcome.

Devotion to consistency is a sign that the brand is about *itself*, not about your donors and their relationship with your cause. It's an approach that doesn't stir donors to action. And it's a strong sign of a brandjacking.

BRANDJACKING WARNING SIGN 6: THE NEW BRAND IS DESIGN—AND LITTLE ELSE

Of all the elements that make up a brand, design is the most visible, but the least important (as we saw in Chapter 3). In a brandjacking, you'll find that the bulk—maybe even all—of the work is a new design framework.

For Brand Experts, design is the low-hanging fruit of their profession. They can quickly transform a brand from ugly and boring to beautiful and cool.

But design by itself isn't powerful. Of all the levers you might use in search of improvement, design is the shortest.

Worse yet, when design sits at the center of communications, you are often forced to twist your messages into crazy pretzel shapes that can't reach donors. Here's an example.

I was on a creative team making a print ad for a commercial client. It was for a sweepstakes, and the call to action was something like *Sign on with us and you'll have a chance to win a vacation in the Caribbean.*

The photo we chose for the ad was pretty obvious: a tropical beach. The thing we hoped people would yearn for and respond to. It wasn't rocket science.

When we sent the ad to our client, the headline sailed through the approval team, which included a couple of notoriously finicky brand enforcers. The photo was another story.

They angrily rejected the photo. "Our brand is all about horizontal lines," they fumed. The horizontal of the horizon wasn't enough. They needed lots of horizontal lines, because that's what the brand guidelines called for.

Advertising a tropical vacation without showing a beach would be somewhat like advertising a car without showing a car. How could we keep the beach but get those horizontal lines?

The brand cops had a solution for us: cover the beach photo with a lot of parallel horizontal lines. It looked as if you were peering at the beach through an office window with miniblinds.

It was almost the exact opposite of the impression we intended: You aren't on a lovely tropical beach, the happy winner of the sweepstakes. You're stuck in your office, staring out the window at an imaginary beach that you know you aren't likely to see any time soon. It emphasized the fact that you most likely won't win the trip. You'll just have to daydream about it. It was one of the most depressing ads I've ever seen.

It was a case of a strongly defined visual brand system that trumped everything else, including the message at hand. (Fortunately for us, it wasn't a direct-response ad. We couldn't be blamed for failure because nobody would ever know if it failed!)

If your Brand Experts deliver a design-centered brand like that, they are boxing you in to a consistent look—and sometimes incoherent messaging.

Good branding is more concerned about communication *than design.*

Good branding is more concerned about *communication* than design. There will be emphasis on copy, and the approach to design will be more about the specific imagery that motivates donors (which we'll examine in Part Three) than abstract design elements like color and fonts.

Brand Experts who tell you otherwise are likely to be brandjackers.

• • •

These are the warning signs of a brandjacking. It's possible with brand work that you'll detect mild tendencies toward one or two of them: The new brand might be a bit more about design than it needs to be. Or there's a small element of pandering to the staff. That's cause for concern, but not a reason to panic.

But the more of these Warning Signs you see in action, the more likely it is you are in a serious brandjacking.

Heeding this list won't protect you from a kidney harvesting. But it could save you a lot of pain and career-limiting embarrassment that would come from presiding over a general collapse in fundraising revenue.

TAKEAWAYS FOR NONPROFIT
BRAND BUILDERS

The six warning signs of a brandjacking are:

- The new brand is not aimed at your donors.
- The new brand requires you to abandon your donors.
- The branding work is not grounded in donor behavior.
- The new brand describes your cause in a symbolic way.
- The new brand requires absolute consistency.
- The new brand is design and little else.

CHAPTER FIVE

Why Branding Matters, and Why It Makes No Difference

Branding is funny. In one sense, it makes all the difference in the world. In another, it makes almost none. Here's a reality check before we dive into the specifics of a money-raising nonprofit brand.

Uncle Maynard is one of the most helpful people I know. One way he helps me is this: every few months, he brings me a banker's box full of charity junk mail.

An eclectic and generous donor, Uncle Maynard gets an epic amount of mail from nonprofits. He's a veteran and gets a lot of mail from veterans' aid organizations. He also gets a lot from local social service organizations (food bank, rescue missions, Salvation Army, and others). Then there are the international relief organizations, conservative political causes, liberal political causes (he's broad-minded), Christian teaching ministries, and more. A lot more.

Uncle Maynard always has a sheepish look on his face when he shows up with the mail. "Are you really sure you want it?"

"I want it," I tell him. Believe me, I want it. Because it's fundraising in its natural environment.

Most of the fundraising messages we professionals look at are the equivalent of zoo animals: rare examples of winning tactics, showcased for their excellence or importance. It's been culled from the jungle of good, mediocre, bad, and really terrible efforts. Maynard's boxes have it all. Most of it is flying under the radar, because it's not the work that makes someone look good or proves a point—it's purely the work of organizations quietly raising funds. Or trying to.

That's how it looks to me, anyway.

As far as Uncle Maynard is concerned, it's a bewildering flood of attempts to get his attention. A lot of it succeeds. Most of the envelopes are open.

Uncle Maynard is troubled by one of the veterans' organizations that write to him. They periodically send him dollar bills. Cash. That offends his Depression-era frugality. He feels forced to reciprocate with a small gift, so he writes a check for six dollars— five dollars to help the vets, plus one to replace the dollar bill. He does that every time he gets another dollar. The organization no doubt thinks it's a winning tactic, but to Uncle Maynard it feels like blackmail.

He doesn't believe me when I tell him he's under no obligation to give—that he can pocket the buck without guilt, and that every time he sends a donation, he only encourages them to do it again.

Uncle Maynard can't bring himself to take the cavalier approach I suggest. It isn't *him*. He wants to reason with them about their wasteful tactic.

The problem is, *he can't remember the name of the organization*. It's one of the many veterans' aid organizations he supports.

That organization has a serious brand problem.

I'm not talking about their tactic of sending of cash.[1] The problem is their lack of distinctiveness. If a repeat donor who pays more attention to their mail than most can't call them to mind, they are a weak, indistinct brand. Maynard knows only two things about this organization: approximately what they do

---

1. That's probably yet another problem for them. It's a high-cost, high-response, low-gift, and (Maynard notwithstanding) low-retention tactic. Chances are, the organization is stuck on a fast-moving treadmill of low-dollar donors, and they dare not jump off.

(which he likes) and one fundraising tactic they use, which he doesn't—though he keeps responding to it.

If that organization were to cut their practice of annoying Uncle Maynard, they'd be left with no territory on his mental map of charities. He'd probably never send them another donation.

If that organization, whoever they are, were to cut their practice of annoying Uncle Maynard with their dollar mailings, they'd be left with no territory on his large mental map of charities. He'd probably never send them another donation. He probably wouldn't even notice that he'd dropped from a multiyear donor to lapsed without a sound.

But it gets worse.

When I asked if he could name *any* of the veterans' charities he supports, Maynard could only come up with one: "Paralyzed . . . something."

Did you just say *ouch*, too?

Standing out is a challenge for any nonprofit. In a crowded field like veterans' aid charities, being distinct and memorable may rival the labors of Hercules for sheer difficulty.

I found mail from 11 different veterans' aid charities in Uncle Maynard's boxes. A few of them are large, prominent organizations that we've all heard of. Most are smaller and more obscure, with niche missions or audiences. The only one Uncle Maynard has ever mentioned to me is the one that annoys him.

No doubt, each of those charities has a clear understanding of how they're distinct from (and better than) all the others, especially those most similar to them. Uncle Maynard hasn't received that memo, nor have any of the other donors who inhabit his corner of the direct-mail universe of donors and prospects.

If any one of those organizations could become noticeable for Uncle Maynard, a small but steady stream of donations would flow in their direction. If they managed to become generally known by the right demographic slice of donors, the fundamental economics of their fundraising program would transform beyond their wildest dreams.

But first things first. What would it take to be remembered by Uncle Maynard?

That's where *brand* enters the picture. That collection of attributes that makes an organization memorable and likeable. They don't have that—at least not enough of it or the right quality to reach Maynard.

A smart friend once asked me this question: "When we talk about 'brand,' *what's the cow?*"

The term *branding* comes from cattle ranching. Ranchers burn a symbol on the hide of their cattle, signifying, "This one is mine." If one of your cattle wanders onto a neighbor's land, you can tell it from his cattle and get it back.

Most people would say your brand is a "mark" that's displayed on your organization—it identifies the organization. That's how Uncle Maynard's dollar-bill organization is doing it. They have a cool name, a well-designed logo, and a consistent look and feel. Bully for them, but none of it is doing the job.

In correct nonprofit branding, the "cow" you should put your brand on is *your donors*. Their hearts and their minds.

A successful nonprofit brand, the kind that Uncle Maynard would be able to remember, isn't a neat little graphic in the upper left corner of an envelope, but an idea that stays in his mind and grows stronger as his experiences with the organization reinforce it.

That's what every fundraiser urgently needs. Without it, you're a bit of fluff floating on the wind, randomly interacting with donors but failing to build relationships.

So get to work on your brand!

But first, we need a reality check.

AUNT EDNA

To those who don't remember her name, Aunt Edna is the Lady Who Complains. She's in her mid-80s and has used her years to refine the art of the complaint to a high art form. (She's only distantly related to Maynard and has never met him. If she ever does, she might become the first person ever to complain about him.)

Aunt Edna's complaining is recreational. She never puts it in writing, and she seldom complains directly to her targets. She concentrates her ire on trivial things, not big ones. She has a debilitating, progressive disease that makes her miserable and will likely kill her within the next year or two. She never complains about it.

You might be surprised to learn that Aunt Edna is a good donor. Not quite in Uncle Maynard's league, but close. The charities she supports are among her favorite complaint topics. In one legendary rant about an international relief organization she's been giving to for decades, she accused them of raising money for a problem that has already been solved *and* for failing to solve that problem despite years of trying.

If you ask Aunt Edna why she gives to charities, her answers will mostly come in the form of complaints: Because the government, the church, or the corporations don't do their jobs. Because it's a way to thumb her nose at various politicians and celebrities she doesn't like. Because it's the only way to get the good tickets.

You can keep probing, but Aunt Edna won't give you any reasons for her giving that are related to brand, design guidelines, copy platform, or mission, vision, or brand personality. She doesn't care about those things. They don't even rise enough into her consciousness for her to complain about them. (I did hear her grumble once about a particular shade of orange. She said it looked like "death." I didn't ask her to clarify.)

I know, because I've asked her. What is it that gets through to her and unlocks the generosity of someone who otherwise seems so ungenerous?

Aunt Edna gives out of habit and obligation. She's done it all her life. When she goes to church, she huffily drops a check in the offering plate. When someone she knows dies, she makes a generous memorial gift to the charity of his or her choosing, even if it's an organization she disapproves of—which are plenty. Most of them, actually.

No matter how deep you dig into her motivations for giving, you won't hear anything at all resembling the concepts those organizations' brand guidelines claim to be the essence of who they are, the lifeblood of their relationship with people like Aunt Edna.

If you pressed Uncle Maynard about his motivations, he might eventually come up with a happy cliché ("Pay it forward!") that's vaguely related to someone's brand ideals. But Aunt Edna—never. Nor will most donors.

No matter how deep you dig into her motivations for giving, you won't hear anything at all resembling the concepts those organizations' brand guidelines claim to be the essence of who they are.

That's because your brand guidelines are all about *you*. They aren't about Aunt Edna. Brands also aren't about Uncle Maynard— or any other donor. All that aspirational poetry has nothing to do with them. They have no more living reality than a North Korean patriotic anthem.

In that sense, your brand is irrelevant. And irrelevant equals invisible. If you hammer it home enough, about the best it can do is rise to the level of annoying—no better than the dollar bills Uncle Maynard gets.

On top of that, the brand you've worked so hard (or paid so much) to develop is probably more aspirational than descriptive. It doesn't quite exist in the physical world—only as a concept in the metaphysical plane of your leaders' (or Brand Experts') minds.

Your logo, your colors, and your image guidelines are not as visible as you think: No matter what color scheme you choose, you are one of a multitude using it. (I know your Mac monitor settings say there are millions of colors. Effectively, there about 12.)

Your copy platform and all the finely crafted talking points that capture your essence—they are all as forgettable to donors as mileposts on a rural highway. None of it really gets through to them.

I'm not saying these things are useless or that you shouldn't work on them. They can help keep communication chaos at bay. They can help align what staff and other stakeholders believe and say about the organization.

But as far as donors are concerned, it's all yesterday morning's mist.

We noted earlier that the "cow" on which your brand should be displayed is your donors' hearts and minds. That's a place you have little control over. Most things you try to put there won't stay. Your look and communication platform won't even make an impression, much less stay there permanently. A rancher might as well use crayons to scribble his mark on his cattle.

Branding that *matters,* that you can count on improving your financial picture because it has a chance to sink in with donors like Uncle Maynard or Aunt Edna—it's the part that actually touches them, especially in these three ways:

1. *The action you put before them.* The specific and concrete ways you're asking them to help change the world (Chapters 6 through 8).

2. *What they see.* The images you use to capture their attention and awaken their passion (Chapters 9 and 10).

3. *How they experience your organization* (Chapters 11 through 14).

Those are the things we'll focus on for the rest of this book.

PART TWO

Your Call to Action

*How Your Cause Connects with Donors and
Brings Your Brand into Their Lives*

CHAPTER SIX

The Seven Elements of a Fundraising Offer

Your fundraising offer, or call to action, is what makes your cause real for your donors.

I was working with a well-known religious charity that wanted more donors to sponsor poor third-world kids. You know—the fundraising offer forever associated with a weepy Sally Struthers. (I wasn't working with the Sally Struthers people, in case you're wondering.) We were creating a series of print ads featuring families who had sponsored children. They would talk about the great things sponsoring did for them for them and for their own kids. I got to interview the families.

You know how interviews can sometimes feel like a verbal game of "Marco Polo" where nobody connects?

Not these interviews. All of the families were fully conscious of why they were sponsors. They were emotionally connected with the children, clear about the organization, happy about what they were doing, and pleased to be involved in persuading others to do it, too.

One thing bothered me.

Family after family told me how thrilled they were when they discovered the child they were sponsoring was a *real person*. Not a fake. It was disturbing. These decent, charitable people had assumed that the well-reputed organization they were sending checks to was *swindling them!* Connecting them with fictional children. This would have directly broken the promise the organization made about sponsorship—a scandalous breach of trust.

Their distrust seemed more suitable for paranoid conspiracy theorists living in bunkers than for involved, good-hearted folks like these. What amazed me most was that they'd become sponsors even though they believed doing so was signing up to get fleeced!

Decades of charity scandals and lifetimes of vague communications come back to haunt us in the form of profoundly distrustful donors.

That's what we're up against in fundraising. Decades of charity scandals and lifetimes of vague communications that didn't put donors in touch with the causes they were asked to support—it all comes back to haunt us in the form of profoundly distrustful donors.

No wonder fundraising is so hard! It's amazing it works at all, given the low opinion so many people have of the charity sector.

What can we do? We can't force donors to forget old scandals. But we can create conditions that help donors get past that nagging fear that they're being taken.

This is why great fundraising offers are so central to a fundraising brand. A fundraising offer is a call to action that will help donors believe what we're saying is true and meaningful and that their gift will make a difference—the difference we said it would make. Give them that, and they won't be eyeing you with suspicion but happily reaching for their checkbooks.

THE SEVEN ELEMENTS OF EFFECTIVE FUNDRAISING OFFERS

1. A problem
2. A solution
3. Cost

(continued)

4. Urgency
5. Donor context
6. Donor benefits
7. Emotion

ELEMENT 1: A PROBLEM

Think of this elemental fundraising proposition that you might see written on a piece of cardboard:

I'm out of work and I'm hungry. Please help.

You don't have to figure it out. Once you read that message, you are forced to take a position: to help solve the problem—or not to.

That is the first step of all effective fundraising: naming the problem. Most people, most of the time, are not thinking about the problem until you put it in front of them. Your job is to put them in the position of saying *yes* or *no*. You start at square one every time you want to motivate people to give. The truth is that most people will say *no*. But that's better than their previous state of not thinking about it at all.

A potential donor needs to agree with you that something isn't right in the world. Something's missing. Somebody is hungry, sick, or lost. A situation needs to change. Sometimes it's more of an opportunity than a problem: something great that can happen if we take action in time.

That is a wide gulf to take people across. You need every creative and imaginative tool at your disposal to help donors *see the problem as real*.

Think about the guy who says he's out of work and hungry. Maybe when you see him, something makes you think he's struggling with alcohol or drugs and that giving him money won't solve the problem he's presenting. You may suspect the problem as he frames it is not the real problem at all.

You may be right or wrong about his life, but either way, *he has failed to make a believable presentation of his problem*. He may have failed because his claim simply isn't true and he can't hide that fact. But let's assume he never touches drugs, his entire problem is prolonged unemployment, and your handout really would help him get back on his feet.

Too bad. He didn't make that case.

Fundraisers fail this way all the time. They undermine their presentation of the problem. Here's how they do it:

- *They downplay the problem.* They fail to make it clear how serious it is, using bland language instead of waving the flag of alarm. They usually do this because they think a strong presentation is sensationalistic. Sometimes they think a clear description of somone's suffering undermines that person's dignity. They should be concerned instead about two things: Is it true, and is it vivid enough to motivate donors to give? (And if you think your little fundraising message can even begin to put a dint in someone's dignity, you're vastly over-estimating your power—or underestimating their dignity.)

- *They're too technical.* Sometimes, they describe the problem in the language of the professionals, not of donors. They're so concerned about technical accuracy that they don't commu-nicate. For instance: Refugees who don't cross an interna-tional border are technically not refugees. They're "internally displaced persons" or IDPs to the professionals. That's more correct, but it's a distinction without a difference. And for a nonexpert, it fails to capture the seriousness of the situation.

- *It's about process, not outcomes.* (More on this shortly.)

- *They're too abstract.* This is the error Brand Experts usually bring to the party. They don't say someone is starving. They say he needs "hope." That may be true. But it isn't a problem that breaks donors' hearts.

And here's the most common mistake of all: They skip mention-ing the problem entirely and just present the solution as a fait accompli. They're making the shaky assumption that donors will want to get aboard with their successful program.

Your donors need to see and believe there's a solution. They can't (maybe shouldn't) give if they can't see how their gift will change things. But a solution without a problem is decaf coffee at six in the morning. It doesn't do the job.

Being good at presenting the problem is not for wimps. It takes guts and an unflinching, eyes-open approach to vividly portray a problem that will motivate donors to act. People on your team who are timid, paranoid, or bureaucratic-minded will not like it!

Your donors need to see and believe there's a solution. But a solution without a problem is decaf coffee at six in the morning.

ELEMENT 2: A SOLUTION

Once you've made a compelling case that there really is a problem, you face another challenge: *selling the solution.*

There's a trick to it, and it's simple—yet somehow it's one of the most elusive things in fundraising: *sell the* **solution**, *not the* **process** *that produces the solution.* Someone who wants a cup of coffee wants the morning fog to clear from his head. He doesn't care about what it takes to move that caffeine from coffee beans growing on a mountainside into his cup and then into his brain.

Solution, not process. When you master this, you are a fundraising prodigy. Or a master diplomat. Probably both.

You have to be a diplomat because most likely *everyone else* in your organization, from the CEO to the guy who fixes the copier, is completely in love with your organization's processes. They don't want you glossing over these glorious processes in your fundraising. Like a diplomat, you have to change their minds, making them think it was their idea in the first place. Good luck!

To keep your solution in the donor's realm, you must show the clear connection between the problem and the solution. It must not be the complex process that sets your organization apart from Brand X Charity, but a simple and obvious connection. Simplicity is everything.

If the problem is hunger, the solution should be food. Even if the way you solve the hunger problem is through a complex process of economic empowerment, civil society, training trainers, or whatever it is. I'm not criticizing your processes. They're good, I'm sure. But they are outside the donor's experience,

And really, your process is effective at eliminating hunger because it *results in food*. Most donors aren't interested in following the winding trail that leads from civil society to a child rescued from the grip of life-threatening hunger. And why should they be? Do you need to know how your cell phone works, or do you just expect it to work?

A well-designed process consistently followed is the secret to success. But that doesn't make the process interesting. The success it produces is what we care about.

Here's an example: climate change. The problem is a buildup of greenhouse gases that's causing an overall rise in Earth's temperature. This leads to rising sea levels and changes in weather patterns, both of which are potentially devastating.

The solution? Decreasing those greenhouse gases.

Did you catch the mistake I just made?

Decreasing greenhouse gases is part of the *process*. The solution is a planet that's back in equilibrium, with less dangerous weather, no prospect of Denver becoming an Atlantic port, and happy polar bears gamboling about on their sea ice. That's a solution donors will see as worth paying for.

HOW TO RAISE FUNDS FOR "BORING" CAUSES

How many nonprofits have boring missions?

To judge by any random sampling of fundraising, it seems about half of them have soul-crushingly dull missions.

I know that's not correct.

I don't think there's any such thing as a boring nonprofit mission. Not all of them stir my soul, and more than a few of them couldn't keep me awake with a box full of party noise-makers. But that tells you more about me than it does about them. Even those I can't stomach have missions that are exciting and relevant—for somebody.

(continued)

So where does all that boring fundraising come from?

It's that way because its creators are communicating with *themselves,* not their donors. They're failing to reach outside their own perception and connect with what their donors know and care about. And that's about as interesting as listening to that weird guy on the bus muttering to himself.

Here's a quick look at the difference between boring, self-centered fundraising and being interesting and relevant to donors:

The Boring Way	The Interesting Way
Numbers: We were founded in 1952 with just two staff. Since then, we've grown to 64 full-time equivalents who serve more than 1,200 beneficiaries during any given week.	*Stories:* The night before we met John, he tried to drink himself to death.
Processes: Our three-step counseling system heals our clients physically, psychologically, and spiritually.	*Outcomes:* John spent years as a hopeless alcoholic, a drain on our community. Now he's free from drink, a good dad, a taxpayer, somebody you'd be glad to call a friend or neighbor.
Philosophy: We believe . . .	*Action:* You can accomplish . . .
First person: I, We	*Second person:* You

To be interesting to others, you have to see from their perspective.

Not everyone has causes like sick children, abandoned puppies, or natural disasters with lots of innocent victims. But let me tell you a disturbing secret: I've worked with organizations with wonderful causes like those—and they were hell-bent on removing those things from their fundraising—because it was so important for them to talk to themselves, about their processes and philosophies.

If your mission is boring, it's your own fault.

ELEMENT 3: COST

You go to a shoe store and find a perfect pair of shoes: comfortable, great looking, right style. You find a clerk ("footwear specialists," they're probably called these days) and ask how much the shoes cost.

"You can purchase footwear for $50, $100, or $250," he says, with no expression on his face.

"Shoes?" you ask.

He nods.

"How much will it cost to buy *this pair of shoes?*"

The clerk scurries away. He can't (or won't) give you such intimate details. You are left wondering how a store with pricing policies like that stays in business.

That may sound like a story by Kafka, but it's the way a lot of nonprofits sell their causes to donors: *Make our work possible.* Just write the check. Donors aren't allowed to have any real connection with what they make possible.

That gives donors no connection between how much they might give and what might happen as a result of their generosity.

An effective fundraising offer connects a problem and its solution with the donor's pocketbook. After all, if you're a skillful communicator and you stir them to care, there are many things a donor might do beyond giving money. They could volunteer, write to their congressperson, pray, or march around with an oddly worded sign. But we are raising funds. We need to get the donor to give money.

A great offer is a specific amount, it "buys" something tangible, and it's a good deal.

Money is integral to the conversation. It needs to move beyond selling shoes (or "shoeness") to selling specific pairs of shoes for specific prices.

I know an organization that, among many other things, provides orthopedic shoes for people with disfigured feet. These shoes cost

$15 a pair, and they can transform someone's life—dramatically improving their mobility and their health. This is a great offer: It's a specific amount, it "buys" something tangible, and it's a good deal. Let's peel that open:

- *Specific.* This isn't a wide-open offer about preventing disability or improving economic output in downtrodden communities—even though it's part of all that. It's shoes. You don't have to be a development expert to understand what they are and what they can do.

- *Tangible.* You can take a photo of a pair of shoes. You can hold them. Everyone knows what they are. No abstract concepts here.

- *A good deal.* Everyone loves a bargain. The best offers give donors "bang for the buck." The strongest offers seem amazingly inexpensive for what they accomplish. That doesn't mean they must be cheap: A $12 million building could transform the cultural life of a city—a bargain!

ELEMENT 4: URGENCY

Delay = Death.

I don't like to intrude into your life too much, but I want you to write this on your bathroom mirror, tape it to your fridge, and maybe tattoo it on the back of your hand. It's that important.

Your working assumption should be that if a donor says yes but puts aside the actual giving for later, there won't be a gift. (That's not 100 percent true. Some donors respond weeks or months after getting your message. But for most, it's now or never.)

That's why a fundraising offer should have time sensitivity built into it—something that makes putting off giving untenable.

If you did a good job describing the problem, there will already be a lot of urgency: Children could die, the building is going to collapse, the matching funds won't be tapped. Make sure you make that urgency clear. Use approaches like these:

- *A deadline for response.* A window of opportunity will close. Maybe the problem will get worse. The more real, connected to the problem, and nonarbitrary your deadline is, the better. But don't turn up your nose at an arbitrary deadline. *Respond by July 15* can be a motivator for someone who otherwise might procrastinate.

- *A holiday or other seasonal reason to respond on time.* Christmas gifts delivered in time for Christmas are much more motivating than ordinary gifts at any old time. And the December 31 tax deadline is one of the most motivating deadlines out there. Use it any time you're mailing around the end of the year.

- *Make sure they know the negative consequences of failing to give immediately.* From your perspective, it may be nothing more serious than keeping cash flow smooth. Your donors need to be closer to the action than that. Tell them in a specific way what's going to happen if the project isn't funded.

ELEMENT 5: DONOR CONTEXT

It's tough to think other people's thoughts. But it's the key to great fundraising. Let me tell you about an organization that thought it had discovered a better way to raise funds than getting in the minds of donors.

It was a large antipoverty organization, and there was a rising tide of discontent among its program staff over its fundraising. They felt that the way their clients (the poor) were portrayed in fundraising was:

- *Too simplistic.* It didn't capture the matrix of environmental, economic, and social factors that trap people in poverty. It seemed as if it were purely a matter of resources: donor gives, poor people get less poor.

- *Too paternalistic.* Because it emphasized the donor's power to change things, they felt it downplayed the role of the poor themselves in their own transformation. It made them look like victims, not the heroes they are.

- *Too sensational.* Even in an extreme famine, there are many people who are only marginally affected. And even the worst poverty zones are full of life and joy alongside the pain. The drama of fundraising failed to acknowledge this.

They wanted us to tell stories and show images of people happily pulling their own weight, succeeding, overcoming, working, playing, smiling. One particularly opinionated and influential staff member said the main image we should show was Planet Earth as seen from space. That would make everyone understand how we are all related and traveling together on this beautiful blue-green ball.

We produced some fundraising that thrilled them to the core: *Finally—you get it,* they said. *This is the first good fundraising we've ever seen!* (They apparently believed we did our crummy old fundraising that they hated because we were ignorant, and just needed them to enlighten us. I sure hope they didn't approach the people they worked with around the world with that attitude.)

How did those campaigns perform?

Do I really need to tell you?

The messaging failed to reach donors. Response rates fell through the floor.

We were talking to the staff, not to donors. That kind of thinking can happen to you. I'll go out on a limb: it *has* happened to you. (It's happened to me.)

Few of your donors are specialists in your mission. In fact, the large majority of them know almost nothing about what you do. And they never will.

But they know enough to care.

Donors' lack of knowledge is not a barrier to their involvement. They only need the compassion to stir them to action. A working technical knowledge of the situation has almost no impact on that. That's why a good fundraising offer doesn't require special knowledge.

When you free yourself from the need to explain everything in depth, you'll be able to state your fundraising offer in *one sentence*. One sentence that contains no professional jargon. One sentence of simple, colloquial language. That means your statement of the offer will fail to express all of the information and nuance that your staff want to see in it.

You should be able to state your fundraising offer in one sentence.

Here's an offer as some organizations might put it:

Yes! I want to help local communities achieve food security through economic development!

That won't mean much outside the offices of the professionals. Instead, it should be:

Yes! I want to help hungry families feed themselves!

Or, better yet:

Yes! I want to help feed hungry families!

The simpler the better. And the more the donor is depicted as the actor, the better yet.

Here's another example:

Yes! I want to make your holistic approach to recovery and self-sufficiency available to all in need.

The organization's holistic approach is no doubt a superb thing, part of the reason they're effective. But it's not the way donors think about it. They're more likely to respond to:

Yes! I want to help young people get off drugs and back into good jobs.

Simplistic? Sure. But that's how you move donors to *yes*.

This can be a difficult issue. Offers with clear donor context are likely to annoy the professionals on your program staff. They may claim that simplification is harmful, that it will depress response. Ask them to show you the (lack of) money. They can't. Because simplicity doesn't hurt response. Really, it doesn't. Never has, never will.

Making your offers pleasing to your professional staff is like burning down the money factory. Donors, not professionals, are your audience. Stay in their world.

DON'T USE YOUR FUNDRAISING OFFER TO EDUCATE YOUR DONORS

I keep meeting fundraisers who want to use their fundraising program to *educate donors*. To show and tell them things about the organization that they ought to know in order to have a well-rounded understanding.

So they deploy fundraising offers with little regard to whether they will persuade donors or not. That's how they intend to give donors a "rounded" picture of the work. They believe it will pay off over the long term as donors deepen their understanding of the organization.

Let's look at the cost of the practice.

Say you have 100 donors. You send them 12 fundraising appeals a year, and you have a normal fundraising program:

- Ten of those have strong offers, with an average response of 8 percent.
- Two are not as good, with an average response of 5 percent.

Over the course of a year, that's 90 responses from those 100 donors. At an average gift of $40, you gross $3,600. Let's say your donors average two gifts per year. That's 45 of the donors giving in the course of a year.

The other 55 donors don't give at all for the entire year: They lapse. You will never again hear from most of them.

(continued)

■ 79 ■

The following year, the 45 who didn't lapse will give $1,600.

Here's how it looks if you use fundraising to educate you donors. The need to educate has left you with few strong appeals:

- Two strong appeals, averaging 8 percent response.
- Five mediocre appeals, averaging 5 percent.
- Five weak (but educational) appeals, averaging 3 percent.

You might be feeling good about the rounded picture of your work that your donors are getting, but here's the outcome:

- Total giving: $2,240
- 56 gifts
- 28 donors giving

That's 37 percent less revenue, which hurts. But here's the big hurt: Instead of 55 percent of the donors lapsing, *72 percent of them lapse*. The remaining 28 donors will give just $1,000 in the following year. Unless you're pulling off miracles in new donor acquisition, this is a picture of a financial death spiral.

That's what an educate-the-donor fundraising program can do: kill short-term revenue and then kill long-term prospects.

And here's the really sad part: Appeals that get poor response are that way because they don't engage donors. They don't respond because you didn't get their attention. There's no education, no deeper understanding. And your cause goes underfunded in the bargain. (You probably lose your job, too.)

If you don't want that, use your fundraising program to raise funds. Donors are in charge of their own education. They don't want—and seldom accept—your help.

ELEMENT 6: DONOR BENEFITS

Some folks think fundraisers have nothing to sell but a tax deduction and a bit of "warm glow." Boy, are they missing the boat!

Giving is packed with benefits for givers. A rich fundraising offer reminds donors of some of those benefits. It raises the value of supporting the cause beyond its merit for improving the world.

Donors are well aware of many of the benefits of giving. Even so, don't miss an opportunity to remind them of the good things that will come back to them as a result of their gift. Things like:

- *Your gift will make our community a better place.* (Or our state, nation, world—it depends on your cause.) Be specific about how they make the community better. Maybe your social service agency will decrease poverty, which will improve the economy and quality of life for everyone. Maybe the community will be more beautiful, more livable, more prestigious, more fun.

- *Help conquer the disease before it strikes you.* This is a motivation for a lot of health charity giving. It may or may not be true—or believable—in your case, so be careful how you make it.

- *Your support will assure that you get something you value.* This is the cornerstone benefit of most arts and public broadcast fundraising.

- *Improve the reputation of your school, which improves your own reputation.*

There are also the general benefits of giving. They can apply to any offer, any time. Look for ways to include some of these in your fundraising:

- Giving is obedient to your faith. (Don't worry, it's obedient to all of them.)

- Giving will make you feel good about yourself.

- Giving is tax deductible.

Selling benefits is almost the sole function of commercial marketing. It's often forgotten in fundraising—a lost art that we should be a lot better at.

ELEMENT 7: EMOTION

You can have all the facts that support your offer lined up like an army on the march, but you'll hardly motivate anyone to give until you reach their hearts.

Blame biology.

We human beings make virtually all our decisions with our emotions.

We human beings make virtually all our decisions with our emotions. Then we circle back with our rational minds to either justify the decision or talk ourselves out of it. It's the way our brains work.

You can watch it happen on an MRI (assuming you're a well-equipped brain research scientist). When someone is making a decision, the right side of the brain—the nonrational side—fires up and goes to work. It's basically examining which choice will *feel better*—create more happiness, more pleasure, more respect from others. When it has decided, the right side settles down and the left side lights up. It's seeking rationalizations.

If you ignore this fundamental truth about human psychology, your fundraising will always be in trouble.

If you don't believe me, try this thought experiment: One of the following things would galvanize you to quicker and more decisive action. Which one?

- A toddler running toward a busy street.

- A white paper about childhood traffic injuries and fatalities.

It *should* be the white paper. That's about thousands of children—not just one. And it gives you context and researched solutions. You'll know a lot more about the issue after reading the white paper than you would after seeing a child wobble toward traffic. Shouldn't that be enough stir you to action?

Of course not. You'd have to be mentally ill to be more compelled by a white paper on traffic safety than a child in danger. That sickening, tight feeling in your torso, that rushing sound in your ears while she veers closer to the heedless cars: It's an emotional, hormonal storm, with no room for rational calculation. In terms of human response, it's the *real thing*.

Yet most nonprofits do "white paper fundraising"—talking to their donors' left brains. It's like going to the DMV to get a really excellent steak dinner. Not gonna happen!

There's often a breakdown between nonprofit professionals and the donors who support them: The professionals have moved beyond the toddler-running-toward-the-street phase of their connection with the cause. They're well into their white paper phase.

They are much more impressed by the scope, depth, and clarity of research than by the immediacy of the real thing. There's nothing wrong with that—it's a normal progression. Their mistake is assuming everyone else is—or should be—in the same place they are.

An e-mail that dramatically and emotionally describes a three-year-old getting hit by a car just seems cheap and manipulative to them. Not a complete picture of a complex issue.

But for donors, the only thing the bare facts do is make the issue harder to understand—and harder to care about.

Of course, when you're raising funds you seldom have a real toddler or actual traffic to stir donors to action. You have the same materials as a white paper: words, pictures, or sounds. You have to make the best of it. The words, sounds, or pictures you use have to be as close to the reality as possible.

MASLOW'S FUNNEL

If you took any psychology class ever in your life, you may remember Abraham Maslow's hierarchy of needs. It looks like
(continued)

this, with "low" physical needs at the bottom and "high" emotional and spiritual needs above.

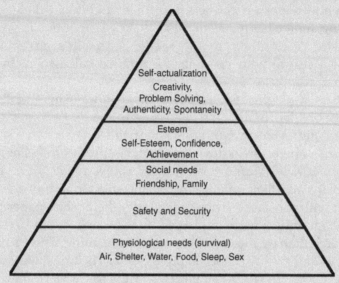

Maslow's hierarchy of needs

I'm not going to argue with Dr. Maslow. But I do have a problem with the way his pyramid is often interpreted in fundraising.

I can't count how many times a Psych 101–educated fundraiser has told me that the "low" levels on the pyramid are in some way less important, less worthy, even less moral than the "high" ones at the top. That strange interpretation of life says fundraising offers that are about food, shelter, or other basic body needs are less appropriate subjects than the nobler needs like self-actualization.

There's a real problem with that: It sets up a false pecking order, as if different needs have different moral value—as if low needs like food are equivalent to other "low" things. As if a food offer is like a crummy pop-music hit by the flavor-of-the-week celebrity, while a self-actualization offer is a Brahms symphony.

(continued)

That's simply an incorrect view of life. There are no value differences among our needs. But more to our point, it leads to ineffective fundraising. The higher you go on Maslow's pyramid, the harder it is to get donors to give. Almost every donor is pleased to help feed a hungry person. Not so many are ready to write a check to help boost the confidence of a stranger.

Here's the good news: There's a way to make Dr. Maslow a friend of your fundraising, rather than a problem. All you have to do is turn his pyramid upside down. Make it a *funnel*. That puts the "low" basic body needs at the top, where they can "catch" the most donors. And it allows some donors—the ones who want to—to filter down to the "high" needs.

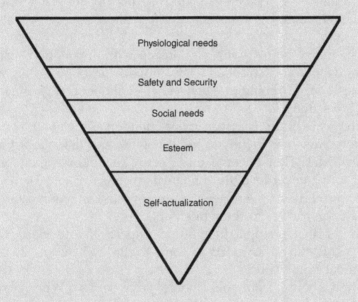

It's no coincidence that the strongest-performing fundraising offers are the most basic. Because our emotions, even though they *feel* complex, poetic, even spiritual, are tightly connected with survival things like food and shelter—and relationship issues, which are also about survival when you get down to it.

(continued)

> - Food is a better offer than food security.
> - Warm meals make a better offer than food.
> - Warm holiday meals are even better than warm meals.
>
> More emotion, more response.

• • •

Something wonderful happens over time when you consistently go to donors with powerful and compelling offers that have the characteristics we've been looking at. It's not just that response gets better (though it does). Or that retention improves (that happens, too).

The magic is how your relationship with donors transforms. It grows deeper and stronger. They move from hoping they aren't getting conned to being true believers—confident that giving to you does great things.

They care more. They pay more attention. They volunteer, offer ideas, recruit their friends to get involved, and talk about you on social media. They become more likely to upgrade their giving, rising to whatever level their financial means allow.

Some of them even get deeply invested in your cause and educate themselves to the white paper level.

In short, the utopia that Brand Experts like to claim they'll deliver (but never do) starts to come to life—when you start with emotional fundraising.

Think about it from your donors' point of view: When a charity they support has meaningful and motivating fundraising offers, they get benefits:

- They get an ongoing sensation that they're changing the world. That feels good! It's a big part of the meaning of life.

- Giving to such an organization makes them happy and proud.

- That organization is probably one of few that treat them as if they matter. It rises to the top of their list.

It's up to us to create these conditions, and fundraising offers are the way to do it.

TAKEAWAYS FOR NONPROFIT BRAND BUILDERS

Strong fundraising offers have these elements:

- A problem that the donor can solve.
- A solution that fits the problem, makes sense, and is within the donor's grasp.
- Cost.
- Urgency to do it now, not wait until later.
- Donor context that makes sense to the nonexpert.
- Donor benefits—what's in it for the donor.
- Emotion.

CHAPTER SEVEN

Your Fundraising Offer from the Inside Out

> Building a strong fundraising offer is not easy. A lot of hard (but invisible) work goes on before you get there. Here are the invisible but important characteristics of a great offer.

In the last chapter, we examined the way a fundraising offer should look and feel to your donor—how it should be a *problem*, its *solution*, a *cost*, with *urgency*, *donor context*, and *donor benefits*. That was the fun part. Now we're going to look at the hard work you have to do behind the scenes to create a motivating fundraising offer.

Remember the movie *Titanic?* We saw the rich and famous passengers basking in luxury. Just yards away from them, completely undetectable, the men who powered the ship labored away in the hellish engine room, dirty with coal dust and streaked with sweat.

That's where we're going now: the engine room of your fundraising offer. We're leaving the pleasant, well-crafted upper decks we've so carefully built for your donors. We're climbing down a series of ladders and squeezing through narrow passages to discover what it takes to make those beautiful offers steam across the ocean of your donor's crowded psyche. Be careful: I just saw a rat scuttling past our feet. It's not pleasant down here. We're going to meet some unseemly characters such as lawyers and accountants. We might even have to talk with them.

But that's what it takes to produce a fundraising offer that does the job of connecting with donors. If you want fundraising offers that motivate donors to give, you have to get your hands—and much of the rest of you—dirty. It's worth the trouble.

FIVE ELEMENTS THAT CREATE A STRONG FUNDRAISING OFFER

1. It's specific.
2. It's believable.
3. It's bite-sized and flexible.
4. It has leverage.
5. It's defensible.

A FUNDRAISING OFFER IS SPECIFIC

Remember how a fundraising offer is a *problem* and its *solution?* If it's a general solution to an open-ended problem, it's not quite an offer. It needs to be a *specific* solution to a clearly defined problem. That's one of the most difficult qualities to achieve in fundraising. And it's one of the most important.

I know you've read dozens of fundraising messages that don't even come close to this ideal. That's because there are two powerful forces at work that keep offers vague. Both are revenue killers that you can avoid when you know what they are:

1. *Many nonprofits can't or won't clearly define what they do.* Defining is hard work, as the next few pages will show you. It takes a lot of information. Asking questions that nobody has ever asked. Doing calculations galore. You may have to work with uncooperative people who "don't have time" to help uncover what you need. No wonder so many nonprofits just give up and ask donors to "stand with us."

2. *Brand Expert "vision."* Their version of an offer is usually little more than the abstract concept of the brand waved in donors' faces. Or clever phrases like "feed the need." Or visual puns, wordplay, or grandiose concepts like—you guessed it—*hope*. Those are not offers. They aren't even fundraising.

Whether your offers are flattened by lack of information or by abstraction, you end up with ineffective fundraising. That's corrosive to your brand and your efforts to get donor support. It plays right into donors' cynicism. It inadvertently says, "We don't really need your money for anything specific." Without specificity, you give the impression that the donor's gift just goes into a giant pot, and it's used to pay executive salaries—unless it's spent frivolously or fraudulently. That's not what vagueness *says*, but the lack of information encourages a cynical donor to fill in the blanks.

You can beat that nasty rap by telling donors how their specific dollars will accomplish specific, desirable goals in the real world. When you supply specific information, you will immediately rise to the top of many donors' lists of organizations they'll consider supporting.

HOW BRAND EXPERTS HIJACKED GIRLS

A few years ago, two interesting facts rose to the tops of a number of fundraisers' minds:

1. In the developing world, a key factor that keeps communities from developing is the oppression of women. Empowering and educating women and girls can transform communities.

2. Most donors are women, and they are increasingly Baby Boomers who grew up in the feminist era. They embrace equality and justice for women more than any generation before them.

The possibilities suggested by this confluence were exciting: a new offer for a new generation—a perfect match.
(continued)

A number of international relief organizations jumped on the bandwagon. You may remember a popular YouTube video called "The Girl Effect" that made a case for educating girls to change the world.

Then the Brand Experts showed up. They saw a great opportunity for politically correct portfolio building. They swarmed the international organizations with stylish, abstract campaigns. They turned the cause of empowering women on its ear. It was no longer a straightforward and specific problem with a wonderfully effective solution. It became a cross between a mind puzzle and a marketing beauty contest.

Campaign after campaign featured stunning photography of stern-looking women or girls, along with clever slogans that were meant to inspire. "I am powerful," says one campaign you can still see in the concourses of down-market airports. An angry-looking woman seems to be challenging you to disagree.

Another campaign featured an animated video in which girls were tossed out of airplane, plummeted lifelessly to earth, and landed on their feet, causing buildings, gardens, and roads to spring up from the earth.

Glorious, conceptual irrelevancies with high production values became the standard way to talk about the cause of changing the world by empowering women.

Most of the campaigns failed. And that's too bad because it caused some organizations to conclude that the whole concept was flawed. The Brand Experts almost killed one of the most promising new offers to come along in recent years.

The good news is that they didn't quite kill it. You can raise a lot of money with offers that emphasize women and the deep change donors can make through them. The way to do it is the way you do any fundraising offer: You show a problem with emotion and urgency. You offer a specific and believable action.

Here's an easy way to think about it: If you can't take a photo of the object or action you're asking the donor to pay for, it's probably not specific enough.

- Sell a bowl of lentils, not "improved nutrition."
- Get them to support a performance Beethoven's Symphony No. 7 washing across a spellbound audience, not "music" or "the arts."
- Talk about a quiet cathedral of old-growth forest, not "the environment."
- Promote cures for cancer, not just support for the fight against cancer.

The mistake many nonprofits make is to think when it comes to talking about the cause, "bigger is better."

The mistake many nonprofits make in fundraising is to think when it comes to talking about the cause, "bigger is better." They believe the philosophical underpinnings of the cause are more important than its specific activities. As if the cause is more meaningful when seen from the 30,000-foot level than it is from right next to it. Fundraising doesn't work that way. No type of marketing or communication works that way.

Suppose you went to the bakery and the guy at the counter asked you to buy in to the concept of the Circle of Life: Everything we are and do eventually returns to the earth, which sends forth grain that's harvested and made into bread that sustains us until we return to the earth.

"Sorry! I just want some bread," you'd mumble as you backed out of the shop. (Don't giggle. I live in Seattle, where we actually have shops like that. They don't last, but new ones keep popping up.) That whole circle-of-life thing is pretty cool if you stop and think about it. But really, even if you do stop and think (which, honestly, most of us don't have time for), you're at the bakery because you want some bread and need to know how much it costs. The guy could have your money in his hand in about 10 seconds if he'd just zero in on what *you* are there for, instead of what *he* is into.

A lot of fundraising is like that bakery. It's selling high-level concepts people don't care about instead of the bread they want.

Don't let that happen to your offer. Be doggedly specific. Not all specific offers are equally great, but the specific ones have a huge advantage over the concepts.

WHAT TO DO WHEN YOUR FUNDRAISING OFFER CAN'T BE SPECIFIC

Sometimes, the nature of your organization's work makes specific offers impossible or unpalatable. Most often, the problem is that your organization's core offer is a large solution to a massive problem: something like *cancer*.

The approach I've been promoting here—breaking out specific, smaller, bite-sized subactivities within the broad solution—may not work when your cause is medical research (or medical anything). Even small parts of the solution are dismayingly expensive. A beaker needed for research might cost $200. You aren't likely to do well going to $25 donors and asking if they'd like to supply one-eighth or perhaps even one quarter of one beaker for a researcher to use in critical experiments. Bite-sized bites feel tiny. One eighth of a beaker seems like no meaningful progress toward conquering Parkinson's disease.

Donors often say, "My gift is too small to make a difference." Your job as a fundraiser is to show them *that isn't true*, even when you have the kind of cause that makes it feel that way. You have to create *a sense of bite-sizedness* in your offer, even for low-end donors. Here are some ways to do that:

- *Address the too-small issue directly.* Say things like "Your gift will make a difference. Every dollar, every penny, brings us closer to the cure."

(*continued*)

- *Keep your ask amounts in each donor's range.* If a donor gives you $50, ask for $50—plus modest upgrade amounts. Do the same for every donor. The exception is very low donors. Someone who gives you $5 once a year is probably costing you more than they're giving. Ask them to give $25.
- *Treat their gift like it's a big deal.* Thank them promptly. Be effusive in your gratitude. Report back consistently and specifically.

Thousands of fundraisers live with this challenge. Some are making it work by seeing things the way donors see them.

A FUNDRAISING OFFER IS BELIEVABLE

One of the good things about making your fundraising offer specific is that it forces you to be *realistic*. You confront the question: Is this something people will actually believe in and pay for? If your head is in the cloud realm of brand abstraction—the "promoting hope" version of the offer—you can easily fool yourself into thinking your own claims are attractive and motivating, even when they're empty and weak.

Back at ground level, with specific offers, you can do a reality check. Does this look real or abstract? Believable or ridiculous? Would it make your mother ask, "Now what are you trying to say?" Or would it have her digging out her checkbook?

DON'T LET YOUR OFFER BE:

- Too big.
- Too philosophical.
- Too much about process.
- Too far from the experience of nonexperts.

■ 95 ■

Make sure your offer doesn't stray from being realistic and attractive to donors in any of these common ways:

- *Too big.* I don't want to rain on your parade by saying we aren't going to eliminate poverty from the world by 2015. Possible or not, it's not believable. Likewise, we aren't going to reverse climate change or find a cure for Alzheimer's in the next few months. But in every one of those too-big cases, we can make meaningful *progress*—and our donors can make progress. Like the boy in the story who was tossing stranded starfish back into the ocean from a beach covered with millions of them, *progress is satisfying*. Even small progress. If the boy had been told to clear the whole beach of starfish, he would have felt defeated before he started. Giant tasks are discouraging.

- *Too much about philosophy.* Philosophy is important, but it's not what donors "buy" when they give. Donors buy action. Every word you use talking about philosophy is a word not talking about action—not telling donors what they need to know in order to give.

- *Too much about process.* Process is important. That doesn't make it good fundraising. Donors aren't interested in funding your processes, no matter how elegant. Donors are buying your *outcomes*. Trying to raise funds by talking about processes is like taking your dog to the park and instead of throwing a stick for him, giving him a lesson in stick aerodynamics. You'll have a disengaged canine companion.

- *Too far from the experience of nonexperts.* One of the things that makes an expert an expert is the ability to see behind the obvious. If an expert visits a community and finds malnourished children, his thought is *not*, "We need a whole bunch of food here!" He looks at what causes the malnutrition: What about the economy, transportation, soil health, or culture is the real problem? With his insight, he might go to donors and say, "There are hungry children here. Please help repair a bridge 10 miles from here." If he did that, the nonexpert donors wouldn't understand. You need to say to donors: "We need a whole bunch of food here!" The fact that we'll get the food there by repairing a bridge is less important.

Fundraising is not for the proud. It's not for those who need to demonstrate their expertise and who think everyone else should be just as interested in their field as they are.

One of the great fundraising offers is the $1.79 meal.[1] It's a great offer because it's specific, it's something that's in the life experience of your donor—and it's cheap (more on that later).

Most organizations that can use the $1.79 meal offer do a lot more than serve meals. In fact, the meals are usually among the least important parts of their programs. But donors want solid, simple, clear offers they can understand. Are you willing to say, "Sorry, Ms. Donor. We don't want your money until you comprehend our programs in all their complex fullness."

That's an expensive attitude. It's one some nonprofits take.

A FUNDRAISING OFFER IS BITE-SIZED FOR DONORS AND FLEXIBLE

The boss said, "Order plenty of bags this time!" Last time, I'd ordered 5,000 paper bags for the grocery store that was my summer job during college. We'd run out too quickly for his taste. So I increased the order to 20,000.

But I made one small mistake. On the order form for the grocery supply company, I wrote "20m" instead of "20k." *M* and *K* both stand for thousand, right?

No. For the grocery supply company, "M" meant *million*. I ordered 20 million paper bags. A thousand times as many bags as I wanted. They wouldn't have fit in the store, even if we got rid of all the groceries and packed all the shelves and aisles with paper bags. The order probably would have required weeks of overtime

---

1. The amount varies; the point is that it's a meal and it's inexpensive.

shifts at the bag factory—not to mention wanton slaughter of a forest or two. Fortunately, an alert order taker called to see if our neighborhood corner grocery really wanted enough paper bags to fill a small stadium. The boss had a good yell at me, and nobody was hurt.

There's a right size for everything. For the store, 5,000 bags was too small. Twenty million was too big. Somewhere between was the just-right "Goldilocks" amount.

It's the same for your donors. If you ask them to do too little, you make them feel underestimated. They can feel as if you assume they're poor or stingy. If you ask for too much, it's hard for them to respond. It puts them in the position of doing less than what you've said matters.

Let's say it costs $1,000 to feed everyone in a hunger-stricken village. Your donor can afford to give $100. She can accomplish only 10 percent of the goal. Going 10 percent of the way feels a lot less heroic and motivating than fully accomplishing a smaller goal—like feeding 50 hungry people for $100 dollars. When you asked her for the $1,000 she couldn't afford, she felt like a failure, picturing how she'd leave 90 percent of the hungry people hungry. But when you asked her for the $100 that's within her capacity, suddenly she's feeling empowered and generous.

To make sure you can ask a wide range of donors to accomplish exciting things within their budget, it helps to have offers that come in small, complete units that you can "repackage" for different donors—bite-sized asks.

Here's what makes this complicated: Donors have different-sized "bites."

The majority of donors can realistically consider giving you somewhere between $10 and $100. If your offer is $1.79 meals, that means you should give these donors an array of choices like this:

10 meals for $17.90

20 meals for $35.80

50 meals for $89.50

That gives the under-$100 donors something satisfying they can do.

But what about that smaller but important group of donors whose "bite" is between $100 and $1,000? You could keep scaling up the number of meals you're asking for:

100 meals for $179

200 meals for $358

500 meals for $895

1,000 meals for $1,790

Is that believable? That's a judgment call. It might be perfectly fine to picture 1,000 meals. But just in case the picture is patently ridiculous, you'll need to recalibrate: Instead of piling more meals into the offer, fund a larger unit, like *feed everyone for a day*. Let's say that's 100 people. That's a unit of $179. So your ask to this fatter-pocket group of donors might look like this:

Feed everyone for a day for $179.

Feed everyone for two days for $358.

Feed everyone for three days for $537.

Feed everyone for a week for $1,253.

It's up to you to make it possible for each donor to make the world a better place by giving an amount they can afford.

Then there are those donors who can easily give you $1,000 and up. Some of them *way* up. For them, you have to abandon meals and go for much larger units. Like:

- All the food we need for a month.
- New kitchen equipment to make us more efficient.
- A new dining hall to make it possible to help even more people.

You owe your donors this level of thought about what you're asking them to do. It's up to you to make it possible for each donor to make the world a better place by giving an amount they can afford. When you do that, more of them give, and give more often.

FOUR WAYS TO IMPROVE YOUR ASK

1. *Have credentials and show them.* If you qualify for badges from watchdogs like the Better Business Bureau, Charity Navigator, the Evangelical Council for Financial Accountability, or other local or niche groups—show them! Make their logos visible. It doesn't matter what you or I might think of the usefulness or completeness of such ratings. Donors look for these things, so bite the bullet and put them out there.

    Watchdogs aren't the only source of credentials that can help donors trust you. Other types include:

    - Endorsements from respected celebrities.
    - Endorsements from other organizations.
    - Ratings or reviews from trusted publications or sites.

2. *Let donors speak for you.* People trust other people more than they trust you. Many donors look for social proof— word from real people—that a charity is what it says it is. Give your donors a voice in your fundraising. This is easiest to do online, but even in noninteractive media, you can have donors talking, sharing their good experiences and why they give.

3. *Be open about your finances and governance.* Freely sharing information says a lot to donors about your trustworthiness. Make it easy for them to see your financial statement, annual report, and IRS 990 forms. Post them, and publicize where they can be found.

    Better yet, go beyond just posting general financial information. Make it clear to donors how you intend to

    (continued)

spend the money they send you. What's the cost break-down of this offer? Why is it so cheap (or expensive)? How much goes to overhead? Show them with pie charts to make it easy.

The fact that you share the information is the important thing. Don't be discouraged if "nobody reads it." For many donors, probably most, the *availability* is more important than what it actually says.

4. *Ignore your lawyers.* If you must have disclaimers, write them in plain English, not in the obfuscatory jargon of lawyers. Legalese is inherently hostile and feels untrustworthy. Don't cover your butt at the cost of coming across as evil.

A FUNDRAISING OFFER HAS A SENSE OF LEVERAGE

The first fundraising offer I remember encountering was this: *A penny will keep a child from going blind.* I was probably seven years old. I was astounded. My earnings were my weekly 50¢ allowance (minus the nickel I was required to tithe into the Sunday School offering plate). I figured that for 30¢ a week, I could help a whole classroom of them every week, and leave a little for myself.

I envisioned dozens of classrooms full of kids, all eagle-eyed and happy because of me. I pictured them going about in a throng, skipping down the dusty roads and singing for joy at the beauty and color they could see.

That offer was probably the cost of vitamin A pills, which can indeed prevent blindness. That offer still exists. It's more than a penny per child, but not a lot more. (Are there children in your life? Introduce them to this offer!)

You don't have to be elderly and frugal to love a good deal. That's why most great fundraising offers give a sense that the donor is stretching her charitable dollar.

The economics of charity often provide us with leverage. Why is the $1.79 meal so inexpensive? The same reason the vitamin pills were just a penny. It's because the organization gets donated food, volunteer labor, tax breaks, and many other things that maximize efficiency. These things provide leverage for the donors' gifts. If you had to pay the full price to buy, prepare, and serve those meals, that $1.79 would rise to somewhere around $12. That's exciting news for most donors. Tell them!

Leverage comes in three main forms:

1. Low cost (such as the one-cent vitamin or the $1.79 meal).

2. Big impact (digging a well in Africa may cost hundreds of dollars, but the positive impact is deep, wide, and long lasting).

3. Multiplication (see Chapter 8 for examples of offers that multiply donors' giving).

A FUNDRAISING OFFER IS DEFENSIBLE

I feel awkward even mentioning this, but *your fundraising offer has to be true*. Sadly, not all nonprofits hold tightly to this standard. That's not you, of course.

Your offer must be not only true, but demonstrably so.

Few donors will ever see the proof that you're telling the truth. That's why organizations are sometimes weak at documenting their offers. But it matters. Remember, a lot of donors (and would-be donors) are afraid you're lying about what you do with their money. Every time a nonprofit is caught lying about that—even caught unable to back up its claims—it confirms their worst suspicions. It tells them they're right not to donate.

That's why we have to be like the builders of medieval cathedrals. They put just as much care into the sculptures and decorations high up on the building where nobody could see them as those down at eye level. The cathedral builders did that because they believed God can see all the decorations. Your reason could be that, too, but also: Anyone at any time, might look at any detail of your offer. Be ready!

Here are some things to check to make sure you have in writing the details and facts about your fundraising offers:

- Are costs correct? If your offer is a $1.79 meal, the actual cost should be darn close to $1.79.

- Is it *still* that much? I knew an organization that didn't recalculate the meal cost for many years. When they finally did, they found it had more than doubled in price.

- Is the money going where you say it's going? If you got donors all excited about saving the wombats, their money needs to go to saving wombats. It's okay if the connection with the wombats is indirect. Just make sure it passes the smell test, and there is no sense that you're getting away with something.

- Is the activity your offer funds real, current, and accurate?

- Is it documented in plain language?

This isn't easy to gather. You'll need to cooperate with accountant types, which can be a challenge. It also might require attorneys. (If it does, please accept my condolences. But you still have to do it.)

• • •

Had enough? Let's climb out of this smelly engine room and rejoin the passengers up in the nicer parts of the ship. In the next chapter, we'll look at some of the best-built fundraising offers out there.

TAKEWAYS FOR NONPROFIT BRAND BUILDERS

What's behind a strong fundraising offer?

- It's a specific activity donors make possible when they give.
- It's believable and understandable even to donors who are not experts or professionals in your field.

- It's bite-sized and flexible so low and high donors alike can see the specific impact of their giving.
- It has leverage—a good deal for donors who want to stretch their giving.
- It's defensible, even under close scrutiny.

CHAPTER EIGHT

Great Fundraising Offers in the Real World

> Here are some powerful, proven fundraising offers being used by leading nonprofits. You are allowed to steal these ideas!

There are probably more good fundraising offers than there are flavors of ice cream. Because, as with ice cream, only our imagination limits what we might invent. Any time you can connect your donor's desire to make the world a better place with real-life activities your organization does—you have a fundraising offer.

Here's a quick tour of some of the powerful fundraising offers that are raising millions of dollars for organizations around the world. You can take any of these and modify them to your circumstances and your donors.

CHILD SPONSORSHIP

Child sponsorship is one of the best fundraising offers ever devised. I don't know who invented it, but that person is the Captain America of Fundraising as far as I'm concerned.

You know how it works: You sign up for a specific child in a poor community, then give a monthly gift. In return, you get information about the child—usually a photo and report, updated periodically. In most cases, the child writes you letters and you can write back.

The specificity of that relationship is powerful. You get regular and believable proof that "your" child is real, and getting helped. Compared to that, most other fundraising offers—where you are helping *somebody* in some way (at best) are pale shadows that only approximately connect donors with the difference they make. Sponsorship gives poverty and its solutions an appealing and understandable face.

I've talked to sponsored children in Africa and Asia. Most of them knew the names of the donors who sponsored them. They were grateful for the support and proud of the connection. I've talked with sponsors, too. They feel even more grateful and blessed. Child sponsorship is a real win-win.

Actually, it's win-win-win: Sponsors are pure platinum in their long-term value to the organizations they support—several times the value of typical donors. If there's a downside, it's the relative difficulty of keeping sponsors if their child leaves the program.

Sponsorship isn't something you can just launch next Tuesday. It requires a complex infrastructure to administer, and calls for a lot of specific expertise. Don't try to go it alone!

Sponsorship has spread beyond developing-world children. You can sponsor a sick or poor Western child, a nurse, a missionary, a firefighter, a dog, a tree. Not all of these have the same power as the original, but most of them have a lot of potential to bond donors with causes.

Here are some organizations that offer traditional child sponsorship:

- World Vision (www.worldvision.org)
- Compassion (www.compassion.com)
- Plan International (www.planusa.org)

SPONSORSHIP LITE

Many organizations, seeing the power of sponsorship, have adapted a simpler form of it, where the donor is not connected to a specific child but to children in need in a broader sense. The donor otherwise gets the trappings of sponsorship, usually in the form of photos and reports of a different child each month. This simulates some of the specificity of traditional child sponsorship.

Sponsorship Lite isn't as strong an offer as traditional sponsorship, and it usually needs to have a much lower monthly donation amount—usually less than $20 a month.

If this form of sponsorship doesn't have all the mojo of the full-fledged version, it does have the considerable advantage of requiring less back-office infrastructure to make it possible. Research shows that donors in this type of program are motivated mainly by the convenience of monthly giving.

Two organizations that offer Sponsorship Lite are:

- St. Jude Children's Research Hospital (www.stjude.org)
- ASPCA (www.aspca.org)

FOOD BANK LEVERAGE OFFER

Every dollar you give provides $8 worth of food for hungry people.

This is the fundraising offer used by many food banks. They arrive at that $8 figure (it varies) by dividing the value of food they provide by the cost of sourcing the food.

There's a real genius to this offer: It takes the uninteresting process of sourcing food and shows donors the end result: Food for hungry people. And it gives donors a good deal. You'd be hard-pressed to raise funds to pay the salaries of food-sourcing professionals who sit in offices making phone calls. But you can get a lot of donors behind multiplying their giving to feed eight times as many hungry people.

A national organization that uses this offer frequently is Feeding America (feedingamerica.org).

SHIPPING

Every dollar you give will ship $30 worth of life-saving supplies to people living in poverty.

This offer is commonly used by international relief organizations. It's easy for donors to understand: The organization has gifts-in-kind on hand—medical, agricultural, or other supplies—and they must raise the funds to ship them to the field. The multiplying figure comes from dividing the value of the donated goods by the cost to ship them. It comes out to anywhere from $3 to around $100 or more.[1]

Show donors the impact like this: "Your gift of $25 will ship $500 worth of supplies." Always do the math for them!

This is a dependably motivating offer. If gifts-in-kind are part of your organization's work, you should use the shipping offer. Your donors will love it and reward you for offering it. A good deal is a powerful force.

Two organizations that use this offer are:

- Good360 (www.good360.org)
- Project HOPE (www.projecthope.org)

MATCHING FUNDS

Matching funds will double your gift!

This is the most common leverage offer, and any organization can use it successfully. Typically, the donor's gift is matched dollar-for-dollar, in effect doubling what she gives.

The sources of these funds are often foundations or government agencies, which earmark them as "matching funds," agreeing to match what a charity can raise from the public. (Foundations and government agencies like leverage just as much as regular donors do!)

 If you don't have these sources of funds, you can build your own. Ask your board members to earmark their giving as matching funds. Or ask other major donors. It is as compelling for them as it is for the regular donors.

---

1. In my experience, the amount of the multiplier has little impact on response. Whether it's $3 or $100, donors respond at about the same rate.

Do the math for your donors, even though it's easy math: $10 will be matched to become $20.

One thing I love about the matching funds offer is that it's almost indestructible. I've seen all kinds of strange things happen to the way it's described: Call it a "match" or a "challenge," talk about "doubling impact" or "doubling the gift." Have a deadline or not. Will the funds be lost if they aren't matched? It's up to you and the funder.

It all works. The active ingredient is that *the donor's gift is multiplied*. The only way to snuff out the life of this offer is to obscure that fact—which is possible if you let nitpickers over-think it.

The only matching grant I've seen that didn't turbo-charge giving is when it's less than dollar-for-dollar, such as *Every dollar you give will be matched by 50¢* or *$10 becomes $15.*

CATALOG

It started with a charming premise: Let donors "buy" a goat, chicken, or cow for a poor family. They'll have food (milk, eggs) and they can sell animals as they breed. It can be a hand up out of poverty. It's so logical and clear. Donors flocked to these catalogs.

Gift catalogs work so well that they've proliferated far beyond farm animals to almost everything you can imagine: building materials, bicycles, medical supplies, books, toys, trees—even high-ticket items like fully staffed schools.

Gift catalogs combine two can't-lose fundraising ingredients:

- Specificity about what the donor's gift is doing (though the fine print in some catalogs makes it clear you can't connect your donation to the gift you choose).
- Choice. Catalogs give donors a lot more choice than they get from most fundraising offers.

Many catalogs also add the element of honor giving, which allows donors to have notification sent to an honoree: "A donation has been made in your honor."

Take these things together, and you have something like cold fusion for fundraising. Little wonder the concept has spread.

Catalogs are not easy to create. They require a distinct copy and design style that's closer to commercial marketing than fundraising. It's a discipline so specialized that catalog marketers have their own professional associations and certifications. Don't tackle this lightly!

Also, printed catalogs can be expensive to produce. I've seen several cases where gift catalogs performed well in direct mail but made poor net revenue because of the high cost. An online catalog is one way around the cost problem. A small, inexpensive "mini-catalog" is another.

Heifer International (www.heifer.org) is a leader in the field. Two other organizations that make good use of hyperspecific offers and the data-sorting power of the Internet are Kiva (www.kiva.org) and DonorsChoose.org (www.donorschoose.org).

PART THREE

Your Fundraising Icon

*The Image that Reminds Donors
Why They Give to You*

CHAPTER NINE

The Visual Foundation of Your Brand

There's one type of image that's central to a money-raising nonprofit brand. That's the fundraising icon.

If you want a striking visual experience, visit an Eastern Orthodox church and check out the icons. You can get a good idea what they're like from printed reproductions, but for the full impact you need to encounter them in their natural environment—the domed space of a church interior, surrounded by other icons.

Religious icons like this sixth-century image of Christ use
a well-defined visual language for specific devotional purposes.

Their eyes seem to gaze back at you. The rich, saturated colors—often including gold leaf—seem to produce an atmosphere that surrounds you. If that weren't enough, most icons employ a technique called *reverse perspective* that places the vanishing point not in the background of the picture, as it is in realistic illustrations, but in front of it, outside of it—about where you're standing when you look at it. It causes a sensation that the icon is observing you.

These things give icons a sense of *reality*, even though they're far from realistic in the way we usually mean that term. Those experienced in the veneration of icons call them "windows into heaven"—windows not only for looking into a higher realm, but through which the higher realm looks back at us, with transforming effect.

Religious icons aren't decoration, nor are they art. They have a specific function: to forge a connection between the viewer and the event or person depicted. The specialized artistic techniques have been developed over the centuries expressly for that purpose.

Since the first time our ancestors daubed plant pigments onto cave walls, we've been using the power of images to connect and learn. Religious iconography is a specialized application of that power.

There's another type of image that can boost fundraising so dependably that it's a key part of any strong nonprofit brand. I call it the *fundraising icon*, because it shares many characteristics with religious icons.

A fundraising icon is an image that employs a visual language to capture the essence of your cause in the minds of your donors. It instantly reminds them *what you do* and *why they care*. It bypasses the chattering, rational left hemisphere of the brain and connects with the side that makes all the decisions—the right hemisphere.

Remember the "poster child" from fundraising campaigns of years ago? Charities would literally choose a child who showed signs of the disease they were fighting and place his photo on posters and other materials for their campaign. They spent a lot of energy finding the child with the right look that would inspire compassion and bring in the gifts. The poster child is a form of fundraising icon.

THE BIG LIE: FUNDRAISING WITHOUT EMOTION

You might be asking, is it ethical to appeal to donors' emotions?

There's an assumption behind that question that we should examine—the assumption that appealing to the emotions is a tactic, something you can choose to do or not do—the way we can choose to use address labels in direct mail, or videos on the Web.

It's a bad assumption, and it leads your thinking (and fundraising) astray.

Emotion is not a tactic. You can't turn it on or off. You can't replace it with nonemotional fundraising. Like it or not, your fundraising—all fundraising—is bursting with emotion.

Human beings live in an atmosphere of emotion. Every decision we make is primarily emotional, made with our right brains. (The left hemisphere's job is to cook up rational reasons for our decisions, after the fact.) Even our most quantitative decisions—planning for retirement income or buying a house—are bathed in emotion and driven by nonrational factors.

All human discourse is an appeal to the emotions.

Fundraisers who think their work does not appeal to the emotions actually do one of these things:

- *They appeal to the emotions, but ineptly.* Even if you attempt to make your case in a completely flat, colorless, emotion-free way, that itself is a type of emotional message. It's the emotion of the unhelpful bureaucrat, of ennui and spiritual deadness. It's unappealing for most people, so it's bad fundraising.

- *They appeal to their own emotions rather than their donors' emotions.* They've labeled their own emotional triggers as rational thoughts and the triggers that tend to move donors as less noble. There's no small helping of arrogance in that. It also leads to bad fundraising.

Using emotion to raise funds is not unethical. It can't be. It's like using oxygen to breathe.

Finding and using a fundraising icon is the most important visual component of an effective nonprofit brand. Color palettes, font choices, and other design techniques are the window dressing of a visual brand. A fundraising icon is the heart.

Your fundraising icon can accomplish everything the Brand Experts claim for their craft—but with two key differences:

- *It really works.* The right fundraising icon consistently and measurably improves revenue, a claim standard branding activity cannot make, as we saw in Chapter 3.

- *Itdoesn'tcostalottofind.* Simple response testing makes it possible for you to zero in on the image that is your icon without guesswork or the high-cost alchemy of Brand Experts.

The most difficult thing about a fundraising icon is that *it won't necessarily say what you'd like to say about your organization.* It's *what your donors need to see about you.* It must be designed for donors, aimed at their hearts and minds. If you try to use it to express your preferences, it won't improve your fundraising. It'll be just one of the thousands of images people see and ignore every day.

A good fundraising icon is memorable and recognizable. When a viewer sees it, she knows what your message is "about."

A good fundraising icon is *memorable* and *recognizable*. When a viewer sees it—on paper, online, even on a billboard—she knows what your message is "about." Your icon telegraphs the core of what you want to say to her in a way that's meaningful and persuasive.

A fundraising icon isn't simply an excellent photo. It's a photo that paves the way to action in viewers' minds. Most images don't do this—and that includes many of the beautiful, emotionally resonant, technically perfect photos that we've all learned to recognize and respect.

We're going to spend the next few pages looking at what gives an image the extraordinary power that makes it a real fundraising icon.

Religious iconographers spend their lives perfecting their craft. Your fundraising icon won't be nearly so difficult. It's a matter of finding it, not creating it. In fact, I'd bet a nickel or two your fundraising icon already exists. It's probably in your files, and you may have used it in your fundraising before. You only need to recognize its special role in your brand and start using it consistently.

Let's look at some of the typical characteristics of an effective fundraising icon. I'll describe the most common characteristics of strong fundraising icons, but we'll also look at some of the many exceptions.

THE BEAUTIFUL ANTI-ICON

Many organizations believe they should display only "positive" images—pictures that show how they're succeeding in their endeavors, like the image below. This means smiling, healthy children. Well-groomed cats or dogs. Pristine landscapes.

Source: Photo courtesy Project HOPE © 2013.

(*continued*)

These images are attractive and encouraging. Your heart lifts and you feel good when you see them. This very real emotional response is what leads many organizations (and Brand Experts) to mandate their use in fundraising. As you seek your fundraising icon, someone is going to tell you that these mission-accomplished images are what you should use.

Donors like them, too. They'll tell you so in focus groups.

But they don't work in fundraising. Photos like this one of smiling children will usually undermine your fundraising. While your words say "There's a need; please give to help," the image says something like "It's a beautiful world; nothing is wrong, and nothing needs to be fixed." And it says so much more loudly and persuasively than whatever your words say.

If a picture is worth a thousand words, a no-problem image is a four-page letter that powerfully makes the case that *the donor's help is not needed*. It can undo the impact of the most persuasive copy ever written. These beautiful images are anti-icons: They capture and display the reason the donor *doesn't need to give*.

There are many places where positive, uplifting images are exactly the right thing. Fundraising is not one of those places.

YOUR ICON HAS A CLEAR FOCAL POINT

Like most works of visual art, a good fundraising icon is strongly composed and compels the eye into itself. I have not yet seen an effective fundraising icon that's visually complex or poorly composed.

And here's the interesting part: Most icons don't show action. They don't tell a story so much as *capture a moment. Or even a feeling.*

Your fundraising icon should have something in common with visual art: strong composition and a clear focal point.

YOUR ICON IS A PERSON

Most fundraising icons are of a person (or an animal), not an object. A hungry child. A sad puppy. A cancer patient. These are images that capture the emotional core of what nonprofits do in the lives of individuals. They challenge the viewer to feel empathy and compassion, and to respond with action (see Exhibit 9.1).

EXHIBIT 9.1

Your fundraising icon is most likely a person—and that
can include animals, like this puppy.

Source: ASPCA web site (www.aspca.org).

The heart of fundraising is *people connecting with people.* Donors touching those they help. A fundraising icon becomes the emotional stand-in for the person your donor helps or the difference she makes when she gives.

Some icons are specific famous or historical people who personify the cause—think Albert Einstein or Helen Keller. But be careful— the person you consider famous may not be recognizable outside the walls of your organization!

Exception: Rarely, a fundraising icon is a well-known and beloved landmark (see Exhibit 9.2)—a natural feature, a building, a bridge, or a work of art.

There are certain landmarks that are not only instantly recognizable but imbued with such "personality" that they almost seem human. The Puget Sound area of Washington State, where I live, is dominated by Mt. Rainier, a massive, snow-covered volcano that's visible for hundreds of miles around. Seeing it

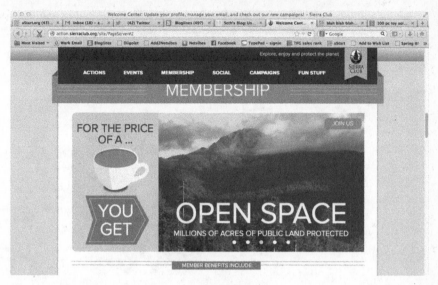

EXHIBIT 9.2

Sometimes, a well-known landmark can be a fundraising icon.
A famous and beloved natural feature, like Half Dome in Yosemite
National Park, can evoke powerful connections in donors' minds.

Source: Sierra Club web site.

is like seeing a friend. Many businesses in the region use images of Mt. Rainier in an icon-like way, and it's on our car license plates.

It's extremely unlikely that your icon is a piece of equipment, no matter how wonderful, important, or expensive it is.

YOUR ICON IS FOCUSED ON THE FACE

The human face, especially when it's making eye contact with the viewer, is probably the most compelling image possible (see Exhibit 9.3). The majority of effective fundraising icons are portraits of people. (That includes animals; any face with two eyes above a mouth has the essentials for making that psychological connection.)

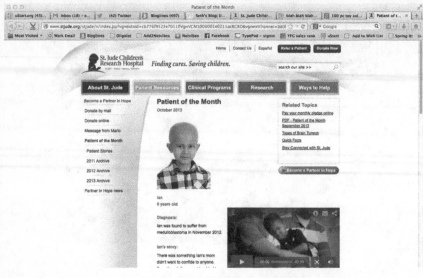

EXHIBIT 9.3

The human face is the most compelling image possible. That's why your fundraising icon is most likely to be focused on a face.

Source: St. Jude Children's Research Hospital web site (www.stjude.org).

Exception: A few times, I've encountered fundraising icons that feature something other than the face: Hands holding a Bible. Feet showing visible signs of the disease we're fighting. These are less common than face-focused icons, but when they're on target, they can be powerful.

YOUR ICON IS ONE PERSON, NOT A GROUP

You may be tempted to use images that show the size of your problem or the scope of your work. Resist! These are not likely to be icons. Many faces together dilute the visual power of the face, and pictures of crowds or groups seldom have that strong focal point that icons have (see Exhibit 9.4).

Exception: One of the most common and beloved of religious icons is Mary holding the infant Jesus. Images like it are good

EXHIBIT 9.4

Most effective fundraising icons feature one person, not many.
Source: Photo courtesy Project HOPE © 2013.

candidates for a fundraising icon if the mother-child relationship has any connection to the cause. A mother, father, and child together—showing a family—is another possibility.

YOUR ICON IS A PICTURE OF *UNMET NEED*

Most fundraising icons *show the problem the donor wants to solve.* This may create a challenge for you or others in your organization, because your idea of what the problem and its solution look can be quite different from a donor's mental picture. You could be stressing out about how to visually depict *low economic output*—while your donor needs to see a picture of *hunger* (see Exhibit 9.5).

EXHIBIT 9.5

While it may be a difficult pill to swallow for many inside your organization, most effective fundraising icons show unmet need.

Source: Food for the Poor web site (http://foodforthepoor.org/).

THE "DANGER" OF NEGATIVE IMAGERY

Can an icon (or an image in general) be *too negative*—so that it dissuades donors from acting? Perhaps the image inadvertently sends the message that the situation is so bad you can't do anything about it.

I've done testing with rough, hard-to-look-at photos, and *I haven't yet found one that drove down giving.*

There's a widespread belief among antipoverty nonprofits that photos of stick-limbed, swollen-bellied, starving children will discourage donors from acting to help fight poverty. That sounds believable, but I've never seen evidence that supports that hypothesis. Those images can be extremely powerful motivators of charitable giving, and some may be good fundraising icons.

(continued)

Whether or not negative images chase away donors, it's clear that they do offend and discourage two groups of people:

- *Nondonors.* Most complaints about negative images come from them. I believe such images throw the price of their inaction in their faces, and thus are uncomfortable reminders of their failure to give.

- *Staff at nonprofits*. Rough images are pictures of failure to them. That's the child they couldn't help. They don't want that reminder, and they are often offended to see it displayed at all.

It's common for images that bother these two groups to be highly effective at motivating *donors* to give. As hard as it can be to ignore complaints, especially from your own colleagues, *donors* are the audience for your fundraising.

And I'll let you in on a little secret: Most fundraising consultants will tell you they've noticed when their client hates an image (or anything else), *it's going to work. Insider audiences provide a surprisingly accurate predictor of success with their dislikes.*

Exception: Some icons show a *need being met* (see Exhibit 9.6)—a hungry person eating, a parent hugging a child, a doctor helping a sick person.

For some causes, it's not possible to show a picture of unmet need. Think arts organizations: What would "No ballet in our community" look like? The icon for most ballet companies is a ballerina—the need for ballet being met.

Another exception: Fundraising icons for disease charities are seldom negative. The icon for these causes is usually someone who visibly has the disease (such as a cancer patient, bald from chemotherapy) but doesn't look sick or defeated.

This might be because so many supporters of organizations fighting diseases like cancer, Parkinson's, or diabetes have firsthand

EXHIBIT 9.6

Not all fundraising icons show unmet need. In some rare cases, they can show need being met.

Source: Charity: Water web site (www.charitywater.org).

experience with the disease. They either have the disease themselves or are close to someone has it. They don't need to be reminded that the disease is terrible. In fact, they may be more inspired to action by the hope that the disease can be conquered or controlled.

However, if you're fighting a disease with which your supporters have no direct experience—such as elephantiasis or leprosy—your icon should show the full impact of the disease.

YOUR ICON IS A PHOTO, NOT AN ILLUSTRATION

Illustrations are not "real"—and they can go terribly wrong. Ever since the invention of photography, people see photos as "real." Reality is one of the key strengths of a fundraising icon.

These have been typical characteristics of fundraising icons in my experience. I would not be surprised to find out there are many more exceptions than the ones I know about. The truth is that each nonprofit organization is unique, with its own unique set of donors. An image that works wonders for one organization could fail miserably for another.

That's why there's only one way to know when you've found your fundraising icon: You must test and let your donors choose it.

HOW I LOST MY PERSPECTIVE AND GOT IT BACK AGAIN

My first job in fundraising was with an organization that did antipoverty work in India. For my first few months, I wrote about a Calcutta taken from what others told me, what I'd read, and a little bit of my imagination. That version of Calcutta was a grim place.

Then I went to Calcutta to experience the work firsthand.

Calcutta (now Kolkata) was no picnic for Western visitors back then. The city was like a black hole, pulling in desperate refugees from the surrounding poverty-stricken hinterland. Political and social violence were common.

The sidewalks were lined with makeshift tents where whole families lived. A tormenting odor of raw sewage, thickened and intensified by the heat and humidity, hung everywhere. Injured and deformed beggars displayed their wounds.

It was worse than the Calcutta I'd been writing about in my fundraising. I realized I'd barely begun to capture the terrible essence of the place.

But after a few shell-shocked days, my picture of the city developed some nuance. I started to appreciate the grace of the people, and to notice the fierce beauty of the crumbling Victorian architecture, to love the food.

The place where I was staying had a view into a walled compound across the street. It was a lush garden, thick with tropical flowers.

One day, I saw a holy man in the garden. He crouched and poured a crystal stream of water over his head from a silver bowl. The water flashed in the sunlight like a mirror. It was a scene of heart-aching beauty that captured my imagination. To this day, that image is my mental icon of the city and people of Calcutta. The place became rich and multi-dimensional for me.

When I returned I home, I felt I had a mission—to teach everyone the truth: While Calcutta may be a place of poverty and pain, it's also a place of transcendent beauty.

Accounts of India that emphasized the ugliness became anathema to me. My own fundraising began to emphasize the wonder of the place over the poverty and suffering. I was embarrassed about my pretrip messaging, which had imitated other fundraising I'd seen, majoring in the negative. I felt a need to atone for what I'd done before.

You can probably guess how my show-the-beauty fundraising did.

It was a disaster. The educated, enlightened posttrip Jeff was a crummy fundraiser.

Not only was I a crummy fundraiser, I blamed the donors for my shortcomings. What is wrong with these people that they don't respond to this rich and important truth I'm offering them? I was well on my way to a life of ineffectiveness in fundraising. I probably would have moved on to some other career.

Fortunately, I found a mentor who opened my eyes to the reality of donors: The beauty of Calcutta is beside the point for most of them. Few will ever look down into that lovely garden. But that's fine. They're giving because they want to combat the ugliness. They need to know the ugliness is there.

My enlightened approach was like a doctor saying to a cancer patient, "Let's celebrate the fact that you are mostly tumor free!" You'd run away from that doctor! If you have cancer, the tumor is what you need to focus on. You need to focus on the bad stuff in order to attack it.

When I realized that, I started turning back into an effective fundraiser.

Since then, I've seen a lot of poverty and suffering all over the world. I know a secret about those places that most people in the West don't understand: The human spirit is so resilient that joy and wonder can flame forth even in the worst places and situations. I'm glad I know that—not just as a platitude or a theory, but as a truth in the marrow of my bones. Maybe you know that, too. You are blessed if you do.

But that secret is not a fundraising proposition. If you put it in front of donors, it will most likely confuse them and dampen their likelihood of giving. It has no more place in your fundraising than would the formula for the ink used to print your messages.

Keep that in mind as you seek your fundraising icon—and every time you try to motivate donors to give. Talk to them about the subject at hand, even though it's ugly, and not about the truths you've learned along the way.

TAKEAWAYS FOR NONPROFIT BRAND BUILDERS

What's behind an effective fundraising icon:

- It has a clear focal point that captures the eye.
- It's a person (or an animal), not an object.
- It's focused on the face.
- It's one person, not a group.
- It's a picture of unmet need.
- It's a photo, not an illustration

CHAPTER TEN

How to Find and Refine Your Fundraising Icon

Discovering your fundraising icon could be one of the easiest or most difficult things you can do. Following these steps will help you be sure you find the right icon that connects with your donors.

In the book version of *The Wizard of Oz*, Dorothy goes to a real country called Oz. It's a magical place, with witches, talking animals, and walking scarecrows—but it's a literal place. She returns to Oz several times (once by a shipwreck), and a few books later in the series, she, Auntie Em, and Uncle Henry (and Toto, too) all emigrate to Oz and settle there permanently.

The movie version is richer and more realistic: Dorothy's visit to Oz turns out to be a dream or a vision, a psychological event that helps her come to terms with her life. At the end, she realizes her adventures in Oz and the amazing people she met there were mirrors of her life in Kansas. The whole thing was a life lesson for her. It's one of those rare cases where the movie is better than the book.

I think of the book version of *The Wizard of Oz* as the Brand Expert version of the story. Because it depends on fantasy being *real*—there is a magic place that you can get to, a place where everything is more exciting, beautiful, and colorful. You don't have to get what you need by schlepping around in the real world, working, learning, and gaining insights the hard way. Just go to the magic land and it's all there for you.

The movie version is more like real life in the fundraising profession, especially when it comes to your fundraising icon. Like Dorothy, you may discover that your brand isn't magic that falls from the sky, but something you've had *all along*—you just needed to recognize and embrace it.

Your fundraising icon has probably already been shot. It's just waiting in your photo file. You may have used it before without realizing what you had. You wake up and see it, and you'll say, "You were there! I saw you!"

Most times I've set out with an organization on the journey to discover a fundraising icon, the one we settled on turned out to be our first or second choice. This points out one of most important qualities of fundraising icons: Like the honest folks on a Kansas farm, they tend to be obvious. Kind of like love—when you find it, you get this *You were here even before I knew you* sensation.

Not always. Sometimes finding your icon is a struggle—an epic slog you'll remember for the rest of your life with a shudder. That's why I urge you to go through the process I'm about to show you—even if it seems unnecessary. It can help you avoid the two traps that can prevent your finding an effective fundraising icon:

- *The too-easy trap.* When you settle too soon. Sometimes groupthink or conflict avoidance sets in. This leads you to make choices that miss your donors. Instead, you choose an icon that works for insiders.

- *The too-difficult trap.* When finding a fundraising icon seems impossible, it may be *your own fault*: You—or someone in your organization—can't see what's in front of you or can't accede to what donors are telling you. It's not always obvious this is happening, so you might begin to think there is no icon for your organization. This process will help you stay focused while you seek your icon, even if it's painful.

(You might ask if there really is *no fundraising icon* for your organization—as if something about your cause makes it nonvisual. That's possible. I've encountered it. But please don't assume that's the case until you've gone through the search all the way through to direct-response testing.)

THREE STEPS FOR FINDING YOUR FUNDRAISING ICON

1. Develop a hypothesis.
2. Put aside your preferences and start winnowing images.
3. Use direct-response testing.

STEP 1: FIND A HYPOTHESIS

This is the easy part. You can probably do it in an afternoon.

Get a group together—smart people who play well together. Make sure your group includes:

- People who know your organization and its work.
- People who know your organization's fundraising issues and your donors.
- People well acquainted with your photo resources.
- People with design responsibility.
- Someone from the outside who's less likely to be wearing your organizations blinders.

For the sake of your sanity and health—keep the group small: three or four people. If you go above five, expect more pain, more time spent, and a lower chance of success.

The task for your elite group of icon-hunters:

- List the common characteristics of fundraising icons you read about in the previous chapter: It has a focal point, it's a person, it shows its face, it's a picture of unmet need, it's a photo. Come to a sense among you what these things mean in your organization's context.

- Look through your existing photos and match them up to these icon characteristics. If you have few (or no) existing photos that meet these criteria, use Google image search or stock photo libraries to find "wish list" photos that are as close as possible to the images you'll need.

- Do this until you have a healthy library of potential fundraising icons. Be open-minded at this stage. It's okay if there are candidate images you think are *terrible*.

At this point, you should have as many as 20 possible icons. It's time to start narrowing down.

STEP 2: PUT ASIDE YOUR PREFERENCES AND WINNOW

This is the hard part. Most people are tempted to go with photos that make them feel good, or that they feel are "accurate" in some way.

If people inside your organization like an image and think it *should* be your icon, it's not the right one. I've been through this drill many times, and the pattern is clear. That's because *you are not your donors*. The images you and your colleagues are drawn to are unlikely to touch them. This pattern is so consistent that when nonprofit employees tell me they *dislike* an image, I think we're on the right track to finding our icon.

The Curious Case of Old Man Eating

You've probably seen photos much like Exhibit 10.1 before. It's the fundraising icon for most urban rescue missions in the United States. I didn't find it. It was discovered long before I was in the business, in the misty early years of direct-response fundraising. To those who have worked with rescue missions, it has a name: "Old Man Eating"—often shortened to OME.

An elderly, bearded male, sitting at a table and eating. This photo is a key ingredient for raising money for rescue missions. It

EXHIBIT **10.1**

Images like this one are a powerful fundraising icon for many urban
rescue missions.

Source: Photo courtesy Seattle's Union Gospel Mission © 2006.

works. It works better than anything else. For decades, missions
have been testing against it: So far, to my knowledge, it's close to
unbeatable.[1]

I'm bringing this particular icon to your attention because there
are two things about it that cause problems within rescue missions:

- The old man is not typical of the people served by most rescue
  missions. Their clientele are mostly young adults and

---

1. I beat it once. But it was a special situation, so I'm not going to give you false
   hope by telling you how!

mothers with children. The elderly typically make up 10 percent or less of those they serve.

- Many people who work at rescue missions are fed up with Old Man Eating, and feel he undermines their credibility and gives their pet hamsters rickets. (Well, not that last one, usually.)

That second problem isn't a *real* problem—it's an attitude, and not a useful one. There's a delusion common in the fundraising profession that anything old and frequently used is *bad*. There's no good reason to believe that. If there's any correlation between old/new and bad/good, it's the other way: The old clichés have stuck around because they work. The new attempts, especially those born from the need to make insiders feel better, are less likely to work.

The majority of new ideas, new businesses, new political parties, and yes, new charities don't work out. There's nothing wrong with newness. It's just that probability is against new and untried things. Most ideas are flawed in ways we don't understand until we try them.

Unfortunately, we can't dismiss this allergy to Old Man Eating, because it's strongly felt in the mission world. The urge to abandon him probably costs millions in lost revenue every year.

To make matters even more vexing, if you ask donors whether it's more important to focus on helping homeless old men or homeless children, they usually say *children*. Yet donor acquisition efforts for rescue missions that feature pictures of homeless children seldom work. OME outperforms kids time after time. (This is another of those cases where the things donors *say* and the things they *do* are completely different.)

The image that touches people's hearts, that motivates them to give to urban rescue missions, is Old Man Eating. Even though he's not the complete picture of the need. Even though these same donors know that helping younger people is more needful. And even though mission insiders have grown to hate it.

The fact that it's the "wrong" image has no bearing. Because the decision to give is emotional, not rational. Emotional triggers, not rational ones, drive charitable giving. And OME is a potent emotional trigger. I've heard several theories why it is, but these theories are not verifiable.[2] And *why* isn't all that important. OME just works. The results prove it: Years upon years of fruitless challenges have not yet deiconized Old Man Eating.[3]

What should you do if you work at an urban rescue mission and you feel Old Man Eating is the wrong image? You have three choices:

- You can stubbornly insist on showing photos more typical of the need and expect "truth" to eventually win out. I hope you won't, though. Doing that will cripple your ability to do your work by decreasing the number of donors who join you. It would be malfeasance. It would lead to more suffering in your community.

- You can spend a zillion dollars trying to "educate" every donor about the "real" problem until eventually a more accurate photo works better than OME. Yeah, right. You don't have a zillion dollars. (If you did, I hope you'd spend it fighting homelessness and poverty; you could put a real dent in those problems with that kind of money!) Anyway, it wouldn't work. The donors already know the truth you want to teach. It's not an issue of knowledge.

- Or you can meet donors *where they are*—not where you wish they'd be. Put forth the image that motivates them to respond, and gratefully accept the gifts they give.

Putting aside your preferences is what separates the fundraising professionals from those who just go through the motions. If you want a fundraising icon that boosts your fundraising effectiveness,

---

2. The theory that seems most credible to me is that it taps into a pool of guilt in many middle-aged and older Americans about underserving their own elderly parents. You know you haven't done enough for your mother!
3. That's not to say you shouldn't keep trying to improve on OME or any working fundraising icon. It's likely that changes in culture and situation could make on this or any icon become ineffective.

there's no other way than using the images and approaches that donors respond to, even if they rub you the wrong way.

Use this hard-nosed, no-baloney approach to narrow down your list of potential icons. Then the fun begins.

STEP 3: USE DIRECT-RESPONSE TESTING

After you have your icon hypotheses, and you've found some images you believe express it well, you should have a short list of candidates. Your fundraising icon is probably one of them. Maybe even more than one. You're almost there.

But hold your horses! There's only one trustworthy way to know when you have a winner: direct-response testing. That means head-to-head direct-mail and online testing where the icon is the only variable—and response is the yardstick.

HOW MANY ICONS?

In my experience, the fundraising icon for most organizations is not one image, but a class of similar images.

If your icon is a sad puppy, many different photos of sad puppies can do the job. As long as they have icon character-istics that work for you. You might find that your icon is any sad puppy, as long as he's brown, has floppy ears, and is sitting behind a fence.

Or you may discover you have quite a bit of wiggle room within the confines of your icon. Maybe the puppy can be any color. Happy *or* sad. Sitting *or* running. Alone *or* with a kid.

This is what you discover in the testing phase of your icon search.

Don't try to get there with surveys or focus groups. That's no better than letting your own preferences rule. Qualitative research *will* lead you astray. It's not possible for survey respondents or focus group participants to tell you what you need to know. They'll tell you what they honestly think they would respond to, but that's not what they will actually respond to.

In the world of marketing research, there are few guarantees. But here's one: *You will get the wrong icon if you rely on focus groups.*

Qualitative research will *lead you astray. It's not possible for survey respondents or focus group participants to tell you what you need to know.*

Frankly, we don't give a darn what people *tell us* about a fundraising icon. Whether they love it, hate it, or have nuanced and well-reasoned opinions about it is of no practical use. We just want to know if an image motivates them to respond to our fundraising. And they don't know—not consciously, anyway.

Here's how to set up your testing: The icon should be the only image visible in any given place. You don't want the wildcard variable of the interaction between images to muddy the testing waters. That means putting the images in places like these:

- On the outer envelope.
- At the top of the letter.
- On the reply coupon.
- As the main image on a Web page.
- Above the fold in an e-mail.

Direct-response testing is a bit like climbing Mt. Everest: It can change your life, but it's not for the casual or the inexperienced. Small errors can have extreme consequences. Unless you have a lot of experience at testing, hire a "sherpa" who knows the way.

A brief word on how to read test results: Don't look at response rate only. Look also at average gift. It's not unusual for a test panel to generate a higher response but a lower average gift—enough lower that it's the loser. Gross income per thousand—revenue per thousand pieces sent—is a figure that expresses response and average gift together, and a good number for making comparisons.

Once testing shows you that you have a donor-approved fund-raising icon, use it. All the time. Use it in prominent places (like the places where you tested it). When you really have a fundraising icon, you'll likely find that you should seldom or never communicate with donors without it. It becomes your organization's face.

Over time, your icon will become stronger as donors recognize it and form an attachment to it. That's when your icon will serve as a powerful and emotional reminder of who you are and what you make possible for them to do.

When you have your fundraising icon, congratulations!

It has more power and positive impact on your fundraising revenue than all the high-end design cooked up by Brand Experts.

TAKEAWAYS FOR NONPROFIT BRAND BUILDERS

- You probably already have your fundraising icon. Now you need to identify it and start using it.

- If you or other people in your organization love an image, it's likely not a good fundraising icon. You are not your donor!

- Let your donors choose your fundraising icon by watching their behavior in direct-response testing.

PART FOUR

The Donor-Focused Nonprofit

How to Become Your Donors' Favorite Cause

CHAPTER ELEVEN

Leprosy or Hansen's Disease? What Donors Need to Know

> Thinking like a donor can be a challenge. You'll quickly realize that the gap between your experience and theirs is chasm that takes effort to cross—your effort, not theirs. Failing to stretch across that chasm can block your ability to build a money-raising brand.

I'd been in India maybe 20 minutes, in a cab from the airport, when I saw him: a small man, sitting by the road, his feet stretched out toward traffic. Something was wrong with the shape of his face—as if one eye and the cheek below had been scooped away. Then my gaze was drawn to his foot. Swollen, mottled pink, surrounded by a cloud of flies. It it didn't look like a foot, more like an underinflated football, oozing, with toenails poking out of it like broken blades.

Leprosy.

In the days that followed, I saw a lot of squalor and suffering. I even saw a couple of corpses. But that man with leprosy stayed in my mind. How wrong can a human life go? How far into suffering and brokenness can someone sink?

Years later, I got the chance to work with an organization that fights leprosy. The disease is completely curable with an inexpensive course of antibiotics. Caught early enough, it will leave no mark, no wound, no stigma. *Sign me up*, I thought. As causes go, you can hardly beat curing people of leprosy.

But there was a problem: The leaders of the organization at the time were dedicated to removing the word *leprosy* from the world's vocabulary. I had to write compelling copy about "Hansen's disease"—and never mention that other name.

That was hard. Kind of like backcountry hiking in slippers.

I could have worked with that. After all, untreated Hansen's is like a torment from the lower levels of Dante's hell. It doesn't make your limbs fall off. It's worse than that. Nerve damage causes sufferers to lose sensation. They get cuts, burns, and other injuries that most people easily avoid or limit. (If you put your hand on a hot stove, you'll jerk it away instantly, before serious damage is done. Someone with Hansen's won't.) Infections spread because they don't hurt. That, combined with clawing caused by eroding cartilage and tendons, is what makes them lose fingers, toes, and limbs. Noses decay and faces are ruined. Blindness is common because they lose the ability to blink, and their eyes feel no irritation. People literally scratch their own eyes out.

But the even greater horror of leprosy is how people with the disease are treated by others. They are often utterly rejected by everyone they know and love. They live in complete isolation, even from their own families. Often, the spirit is even more damaged by leprosy than the body.

Call it leprosy or call it Hansen's disease—I had a story to tell.

But I couldn't.

Eliminating the word *leprosy* was only part of the organization's crusade. They believed that we played into the stigma of leprosy any time we zeroed in on its harmful effects. As far as they were concerned, focused descriptions of people with Hansen's disease were no different from the rocks and cruel insults that are hurled at them.

The things I've just told you would have been out of the question. We were enjoined instead to tell hope-filled stories of patients who bravely made lives for themselves despite disabilities. Or people who'd been cured early and now lived normal lives.

As you can probably imagine, getting donors to rally around the cause of helping healthy people who used to have a disease nobody has ever heard of was a bit rough. In a world where children have cancer, people are homeless, earthquakes flatten cities, puppies are abused, and the polar ice caps are melting, who has the bandwidth for an obscure disease that apparently poses no meaningful threat to anyone?

You won't be shocked to know that the organization was in steep financial decline. Their fundraising just didn't work. Working on their projects, I felt like a baseball player stepping up to the plate and having the pitcher hurl a Nerf ball into my strike zone. It didn't matter how hard I swung.

I understand those Hansen's disease professionals. Their approach was rooted in compassion. Hansen's disease wasn't just a "cause" for them—they worked among patients, knew them personally, felt their agony. They didn't want to wallow in that pain and exploit it. When they looked at one of their patients, they saw a human being, not a disease. They wanted the whole world to see it that way.

They were choosing to deny donors the very information that had transformed their own lives.

They knew an important truth: that even the most terribly afflicted person is not defined by his illness. If you or anyone close to you has battled a serious disease, you know this, too.

But there's another truth they were missing, one more apropos to the situation at hand: *You can't make people care about something that's abstract to them.*

Leprosy is outside of nearly every donor's experience.[1] Beyond a few biblical stories about miraculous healings, there's no leprosy in anyone's memory. So if you neither name the disease nor describe its horrors, you will never carry people into the place where they know enough to care—or care enough to give.

---

1. About 100 Americans contract leprosy each year. You can get it from armadillos.

These professionals were choosing to deny donors the very information that had transformed their own lives—the stories and images that sent them down a path to becoming heroes in the fight against leprosy.

They were keeping donors in the dark because *it felt better for them that way*. Like many nonprofit professionals, they were unable to get outside of their own heads.

This is a defining struggle for many nonprofits, especially those that help people who are poor, sick, or otherwise suffering. They know the horrors they're fighting. They know them more deeply and clearly than you or I ever will. But they've moved on to a different place, a place where looking at horrors is superfluous, even harmful, to a meaningful understanding of the issue.

They're like good soldiers who fought, who crawled through the mud with bullets whistling just over their heads—until they were promoted. Now they fight from conference rooms in the Pentagon. Those well-ordered chambers are critical to the war effort, but the mud-and-bullets side of war is what most people think of as the real thing.

Donors aren't with us in the conference rooms *or* on their faces in the mud. Most of them will never be there.

When nonprofit professionals mandate "professional" ways of describing their issues, they make a choice: to motivate fewer donors, raise less revenue, and do less good.

And there's nothing wrong with those "shallow" donors. They can support your cause wholeheartedly if they catch the vision. Those "shallow" donors make the philanthropic world go 'round. Their less advanced understanding is no barrier to giving. The barrier is weak fundraising that fails to meet them where they are.

When nonprofit professionals mandate abstract, "professional" ways of describing their issues in their fundraising, they make a choice: to motivate fewer donors, raise less revenue, and do less good. And that, as far as I'm concerned, is way too high a price for being able to feel good about your fundraising. To put it bluntly: How many people still have leprosy because some people refused to say *leprosy?*

That refusal to connect with real-life donors is one of the differences between an ineffective fundraising brand and a brand that powers fundraising. And the ability to get outside of your own head and talk to donors, rather than to yourself, is the first and most important step to a donor-focused brand.

FIVE WAYS NONPROFITS DRIVE AWAY THEIR DONORS

I haven't yet encountered a nonprofit organization that wanted fewer donors, or donors who care less, give less, and badmouth the organization to their friends.

I've met a few, though, that act as if that's exactly what they want.

In case you're looking to shed some donors (or maybe you'd like to avoid doing that), here are some common nonprofit practices that drive donors away:

FIVE WAYS TO DRIVE AWAY DONORS

1. Write and design for your coworkers.
2. Change the subject between your acquisition and cultivation messages.
3. Educate your donors.
4. Develop your web site differently from your offline messages.
5. Have sloppy donor data.

Drive Away Donors by Writing and Designing for Your Coworkers

We've discussed elsewhere the danger of aiming your messages at yourself rather than your donors. There's an even more insidious way to miss your donors: create fundraising that pleases your professional colleagues.

It's a strong temptation, and many fall to it. Because you have to face your coworkers every day. If your work annoys them, you have to live with their complaints and reproaches.

By comparison, donors don't cause you pain: If your work fails to connect with them, you won't hear complaints. They'll just respond less. That's the ultimate failure for a fundraiser, but let's be honest: lower response doesn't feel that bad while it's happening. You can't even tell it's happening. The pain starts much later.

Failing to satisfy your colleagues is like touching a live wire and getting an immediate shock. Failing to satisfy donors is like eating too much junk food and feeling the impact on your health months or years later.

Let's be clear: Poor response will happen when you aim to please your colleagues. What works for them *won't work* for donors. It's too detailed, too educated, requires too much background knowledge, and it's probably too modern in style—those are all qualities that kill fundraising.

On the other hand, what works for your donors will drive your colleagues crazy. They'll find it too simplistic, too emotional, too *"bleagh,"* as I've heard it carefully described several times.

These two mind-sets—professional and donor—will never meet. And there's no compromise. Your fundraising can miss your colleagues, or it can miss your donors. The compromise is something that misses both.

This is an unavoidable fact of life for nonprofits. The sooner you can persuade your fellow insiders to stop expecting your fundraising to make them happy, the sooner you'll have peace. And effective fundraising.

Drive Away Donors by Changing the Subject

If you make disciplined use of any direct-response channels to acquire donors, you probably have a fine-tuned new donor acquisition message. All the wishful thinking, fuzzy writing, ill-conceived ideas, and confusing calls to action have been strained out by testing. It gets through to donors with a sharp and concise offer. It's a fundraising dynamo that powers your program by bringing donors who grasp the message and respond generously. An effective fund-raising control is an asset of almost incalculable value. Even if it vanished into thin air today, it would keep on paying dividends for years to come as the donors it brought in continue to give.

Want to know something a little crazy? Many organizations that have a strong acquisition control never again send those donors an offer or message that's like the one that brought them on board. Instead, they get offers the organization feels better about—less specific, less urgent, and less clear.

When you switch from a strong acquisition offer to a weak cultivation one, you are playing a version of that old con-artist game, bait and switch.

It's a terrible disconnect. I imagine donors asking, "Why did you change the subject?" More likely, the change of subject just causes them to lose track of who you are. You slip noiselessly from their "causes I support" category onto their much larger "causes I don't remember anything about" category.

The consequences are poor campaign results and low donor retention. It's a double-whammy that kills revenue in the short and long terms.

When you switch from a strong acquisition offer to a weak cultivation one, you are playing a version of that old con-artist game, bait and switch.

Ask yourself how you'd feel if you wanted to go on a ski vacation, so you found a really great ski resort and booked it, but when you got there, it was a wine resort. The resort owners preferred wine-tasting over skiing and expected you go along with their preferences.

Don't do that to donors. It's rude, and it will crush donor retention.

Drive Away Donors by Educating Your Donors

The temptation to mold your donors into better people (that is, people who think and act like *you*) is a strong one. After all, your donors know a lot less about the cause than you do, and a little extra knowledge would only deepen their connection with you. Right?

Well, no. Educating people and motivating people to give are radically different activities. The two things happen in different parts of the brain, under different circumstances, and through different types of relationships. It might as well be in different galaxies.

If your fundraising is aiming to educate donors, then it isn't really fundraising, any more than your graduate thesis would have made a good love letter.

Donors don't want (or need) to be educated. Hardly anyone wants to be educated. I used to be a teacher, and I can tell you that even college students who are paying good money to be educated and are dedicating important years of their life to the project can barely tolerate being taught.

Your donors are even less inclined to receive your teaching. They aren't paying you tuition. They aren't sitting in a classroom. More likely, they're sorting their mail over the recycle bin, or going through their inbox with a heavy finger on the delete key. Try to sneak an unwanted bit of curriculum past them, and you're gone.

A small number of your donors will catch the bug for your cause and seek to deepen their knowledge about it. You'll find them, or they'll find you, and you'll probably enjoy the relationship.

But most donors aren't interested. There's nothing wrong with that. Their money is just as good, even if they remain "ignorant."

ARE YOU A DONOR?

If you're a fundraiser, and you don't give to charities yourself, you are only *half a fundraiser*. Maybe less. You'll never be fully effective. You may be blessed with intelligence, imagination, and insight—but a fundraiser who isn't a donor is no better than a parrot, or a machine.

Charitable giving is an act of the heart. And the heart, as Pascal noted, has its reasons of which reason knows nothing. If your heart is inexperienced in the act of giving, the entire enterprise of fundraising and giving will be opaque to you. Donors live in the Garden; you inhabit a sterile office cubicle. The ways they think and act are almost meaningless to you.

That's why nondonor fundraisers are prone to bone-headed errors of judgment and perception. The most common error is thinking *donors don't like to give.* They assume that fundraising is a zero-sum game, where we remove resources from donors, leaving us enriched and donors depleted and annoyed. That's not at all what happens! If you're a donor, you know you're out a few bucks after giving, but in every other way, the ways that matter, you get the sweeter end of the deal.

A second common error is thinking fundraisers should "teach" donors into giving, that we should avoid messy, untrustworthy emotional appeals. These fundraisers adapt a cool, journalistic, detached style of fundraising. They have no idea how irrelevant and off-putting it is.

Both of these errors lead to not asking enough, not asking with passion and clarity, and failing to connect with what really makes donors give.

These are basic, revenue-crushing errors that happen all the time. Fundraisers who don't participate make these errors again and again. They can't properly diagnose their short-comings, so they often enter feedback loops that drive their results down: They think donors aren't giving because the fundraising is too emotional . . . so they make it less emotional . . . so the donors respond less. It goes around and around, getting worse as it goes.

If that's you, it's time to take the step and start giving.

If your income is low, give small amounts. If you don't have a cause you love, find one you like. It's smart to give to your own organization, but it's not necessary. Just give.

It will change your fundraising. And your life.

Drive Away Donors by Developing Your Web Site Differently from Your Offline Messages

Donors don't stay obediently within the communication channels we set out for them. They use the channels *they* prefer and in the ways *they* want to. It makes life difficult for us, but that's the way they do it now.

This behavior especially matters in direct mail, because so many donors combine the Web with the mail to complete their giving. Some go online to find out whether they want to give, then return to the mail for the gift. Many direct mail recipients give online. This "web site two-step" is becoming almost standard donor behavior. So you should ask yourself: Does your web site help donors do what they want to do, or does it block and confuse them?

THREE THINGS YOUR DONORS SHOULD BE ABLE TO FIND ON YOUR WEB SITE

1. Information that tells them they can trust you.
2. A clear statement of what you do.
3. Easy-to-use donation form.

Here are three common ways nonprofit web sites fail to help channel-hopping donors:

- *The web site has a radically different look, feel, personality, and message than the offline message that sent them to the site.* Many web sites are developed in such isolation from working direct-response channels that even the most attentive donors can't tell that they're looking at the same organization.

- *It's hard for donors to find the information they're looking for.* Information that tells them they can trust you (such as efficiency and effectiveness statement and third-party endorsements from watchdog organization or other sources they trust), a clear statement of what you do, and an easy-to-use donation form that's related to the mail that got them excited enough to seek you out. These three things should be so easy to find, a mole could spot them in a dense fog. If they aren't, you are losing donors and their gifts.

- *There's too much going on.* Many web sites exist not only to raise funds but also to sell tickets, recruit patients, serve constituents, provide information, and more. There's not an easy solution to this, but top-notch Web design, tested and optimized for user experience, is critical. Or perhaps your fundraising should happen on a web site of its own, separate from other agendas.

Drive Away Donors by Having Sloppy Donor Data

Probably the closest a nonprofit can come to being as evil and annoying as a cell phone company or an airline (like Amalgamated Air) is by mishandling donor data.

If you have multiple names or addresses for the same donor, you are sending a clear message: *you are not important* and/or *we are not competent.* If a gift is not correctly recorded, you signal that the gift doesn't matter much.

Being a donor to your organization should be a smooth, stress-free, no-error experience. Anything less will cost you in donor loyalty and retention.

I'm grateful that most nonprofits lack the capacity or position to torment their donors the way some businesses do to their customers. Please be careful not even to get close to the bad practices that darken so many customer relationships.

• • •

In the next few chapters, we'll look at what it takes to focus on donors. We'll look first at the ways to tell stories that matter to donors and what to communicate so you motivate. Then we'll look at the philosophy and systems of running an organization that serves donors in ways they need to be served so they can be committed, connected donors who stay for the long haul.

But first, let me tell you what happened with the leprosy organization: I'm happy to say they recovered from their Hansen's disease folly. They now show photos and tell stories about people with leprosy. Honestly, it makes them uncomfortable sometimes. But they're able to live with the discomfort because they know what really matters—helping people with leprosy—is getting the funding it needs.

TAKEAWAYS FOR NONPROFIT BRAND BUILDERS

- You can't make people care about something that's abstract to them.
- You'll never be a fully developed fundraiser unless you are also a donor.
- Don't create fundraising messages that resonate with you or your professional colleagues.
- Your donor acquisition and donor cultivation messages should be similar in offer, subject, and tone. Otherwise, you'll have trouble keeping donors.
- Don't try to educate donors into giving. Inspire them.
- Make sure your web site and your online messages are closely integrated.

CHAPTER TWELVE

Communicating as if Donors Mattered

Putting donors first is just an empty slogan unless you practice "Golden Rule" fundraising that actually puts them first. This chapter shows you some solid steps for connecting with donors in ways that are meaningful to them.

Dale Carnegie knew it. Buddha knew it. So did Jesus. So has every likable, influential person you can think of. Heck, I'll bet your mother knew it—she probably even told you about it.

This is what they all knew: The best way to treat other people is to care about them and treat them right. Be interested in them. Listen to them. *Put their concerns ahead of your own.*

Knowing that (and acting on it) can revolutionize any relationship. It works between people, between organizations, and when people interact with organizations. It can solve almost any problem. It's so universally valuable, it is sometimes called the Golden Rule.

If you practice the Golden Rule with someone, you have more influence with them. They'll like you, trust you, and listen to you.

Sadly, some nonprofits communicate and raise funds as if they've never heard of the Golden Rule. Their communication platform is decidedly self-focused: *Tell our story! Show everyone how awesome we are.* Some even take it down a darker path: *Donors are inferior, and we must improve them.*

Fundraising that way is a soul-sapping, money-wasting struggle. Because it never works. But it's common. Us-first, tell-our-story fundraising might be one of the reasons so many studies and surveys find that a high percentage of nonprofit professionals are unhappy and want to leave their jobs.

Fundraising that ignores the Golden Rule could be called the *Awesome Nonprofit* approach, because it's built on the assumption that if you brag well enough, people will want to give. Awesome Nonprofit fundraising does a better job making insiders feel good than it does at raising funds. It's also the empty heart beneath the optimistic promises Brand Experts make to nonprofits: *We'll create a magic formula that will show everyone how awesome you are! Then they'll all give to you!*

But they won't. People aren't that interested in how great you are. That's why Awesome Nonprofit fundraising is the path to failure.

Please don't think I'm saying you shouldn't *be* awesome. I hope you're over-the-top, best-thing-since-sliced-bread awesome. I hope the most elaborate puffery the Brand Experts could ever cook up for you falls sadly short of your true excellence. You owe that to your cause, your donors, and yourself.

But don't make your awesomeness a fundraising platform. Going on about how superb you are is just as insufferable when it's an organization doing it as when a self-centered braggart corners you at a party and does it.

The fundamental truth about why people donate to any organization is this:

Donors don't give because you are great. They give because they are great.

When you know this truth and let it drive your communications, you are a *real fundraiser*. And that's a big deal, because the difference between an Awesome Nonprofit fundraiser and a Golden Rule fundraiser is like the difference between a plasticky televangelist and a real prophet.

Here's how the two platforms express themselves to donors:

- *Awesome Nonprofit:* We're so great, the best move you could make right now would be to hitch your wagon to our star. We'll use your gift to do incredible things that will thrill you!

- *Golden Rule:* You are a great person. You get it. That's why we'd love to hitch our wagon to your star so we can do thrilling things together.

★ HALLMARKS OF DONOR-FOCUSED COMMUNICATIONS

- Donors are the heroes of most stories.
- Donors get prompt, detailed, and frequent information on the impact of their giving.
- Donors have control over how you communicate with them.
- Design is appropriate for donors—not aimed at internal audiences.

When you focus on donors, you don't hide your excellence. You share facets of greatness as they relate to the donor. Make it clear your excellence is one of the reasons she should choose you as her partner in *her mission.* Your greatness is an extension of her greatness. Don't turn it into a laundry list that's meant to browbeat the donor into accepting the inevitable fact that you are so great she *must* donate.

Let's look at how putting donors first can play out in real-life donor communications: First we'll examine the stories you tell (and how you tell them). Then we'll focus on the importance of reporting back to donors about their giving and the right way to design for a donor. Finally, we'll look at how to measure your efforts so you can be sure you're getting it right.

WHY BAD FUNDRAISING WORKS

As someone who cares about fundraising, you may have noticed something: There's a lot of truly terrible fundraising out there: sloppy, vague, full-of-itself, donor-blind fundraising.

It persists because it works. If it didn't, there'd be much less of it.

Bad fundraising works because of a curious truth: *Bad fundraising works because of good donors.*

Donors want to give. Some are so determined to give, they do the work bad fundraisers fail to do. They fill in what the fundraisers left out, and then respond.

When there's no clear call to action, some donors imagine one of their own.

When there's no story, some donors author a wonderful, donor-focused story that makes them want to give.

When the images are off-target, some donors visualize the right images, drawing from pictures they've seen elsewhere or from their life experience.

With help like that, it's hard to go wrong.

Which can be just plain discouraging if you're a fundraiser who cares about quality and works hard to get it right.

Don't despair. Your excellence matters: Bad fundraising works less well all the time.

The demographic group most likely to do bad fundraisers' jobs for them are those we call the World War II or "Silent" generation: people born between around 1920 and 1945. These people are strongly motivated by duty, and they know they have a duty to give. But they are disappearing. Every day, more members of the WWII generation die. And every day in the United States, they are replaced by 7,000 more demanding, more skeptical Baby Boomers (the pattern is similar throughout the Western world).

(continued)

These Boomers are less likely to rewrite bad fundraising into good. They're too skeptical to do that.

These Boomers now make up a slight and fast-increasing majority of the 55–85 population in the United States—that is, the prime donor age.

Organizations that have skated by with bad fundraising because they have good donors face hard times in the coming years. Anyway, even with the most angelic do-your-job-for-you donors, good fundraising works better than bad.

Don't be discouraged when you see bad fundraising. It is an endangered species.

DONOR-FOCUSED STORIES

Everyone who's paying attention knows that storytelling is the best way to motivate people to give. Facts and statistics don't connect with your donors' hearts and don't move them to action.

But let's take a deeper look at that well-known truth. Because not all stories are equal. Some do all the great things stories are supposed to do. Others are flat, revenue-killing duds you'd be better off without—no better than a bullet list of statistics.

It's a matter of who the hero is.

The central element of any story is its *hero*. A story is hardly a story at all if it doesn't feature a hero: the central figure in your story. The person (it's not always an individual, and it's not always a human being) who matters most in the story. The one everything important happens to and/or the one who does the important things.

Here are three types of fundraising stories with different heroes and how they connect with donors.

1. *The nonprofit as hero*
   It goes like this: *We were founded in 1948 by a genius who invented our dynamic, cutting-edge methodologies. And our*

excellent staff are the best! You've seen this type of story many times, right?

When the nonprofit is the hero, the story is mainly bragging. Empty bragging. It has little impact on people, because it isn't interesting. Think about it: We all swim in a sea of boastful claims (by commercial marketers, mostly). Does anyone want to hear yet another "We are the best"proclamation? Will anyone even believe it?

You may be technically telling a story when your organization is the hero, but it has little power to stir the heart. And it almost never works in fundraising. Don't waste your time telling stories with your organization as the hero!

2. *A beneficiary as hero*

This is the story most fundraisers who are paying attention want to tell. It goes like this: *The day Hannah learned she was HIV-positive was the worst day of her life.*

At its best, a beneficiary story offers emotional and believable proof that the work is needed. But even when it's powerful, interesting, and relevant—it doesn't necessarily connect with the donor. It's just a story.

A beneficiary-as-hero story is not the guaranteed winner people make it out to be. It works in fundraising when the pure drama and relevance make it stand out among the hundreds of stories your donor will encounter the day she sees yours. Then, it might do the job and motivate a gift. But there's a much better hero you should build your stories around. . . .

3. *The donor as hero*

This is the story the real fundraising pros tell. It goes like this: *Some people can't stand to hear about the spread of tuberculosis. It makes them feel powerless and depressed. Not you. You read about this deadly disease, and you know you can help change the situation.*

Usually (not always), a donor-as-hero story has a beneficiary in it. But it's told in a way that makes the donor a part of the action: Hannah may be HIV-positive, but she has hope because the donor cares enough to reach out generously.

[handwritten note in margin: COTN does this a lot]

Donor-as-hero stories usually work in fundraising. They're as close to a slam-dunk fundraising technique as you'll find.

You move away from the temptation to impress with your five-star creative writing ability and toward simply communicating with your reader.

A wonderful thing happens to your writing when you tell a donor-as-hero story. It gets less "writerly" and more conversational. You move away from the temptation to impress with your five-star creative writing ability and toward simply communicating with your reader. You use the word *you* a lot. Your style gets more like a letter and less like something from a creative writing workshop.

This baffles some nonprofits. They may think, "What the heck? I hire a professional writer and his copy sounds like my Aunt Ruth!" But the verbal fireworks they're looking for (and that you can count on many writers to produce) is not the best style for fundraising. And here's a secret: Writing so you sound genuinely like Aunt Ruth is much more difficult to master than writing like an over-caffeinated Hemingway.

Here's the colloquial Aunt Ruth writing style I'm talking about:

Dear Mrs. Donor:

Just [time since last donation] ago, you sent a gift of [last donation amount]. Your gift is now hard at work saving lives and keeping children safe in the inner city. Thank you so much for caring!

It doesn't have the taut rhythm, explosive verbs, and souped-up details of "creative" writing. But it sounds real. And it's about the donor. Sounding real and writing about the donor are the killer tactics of fundraising.

THE CURSE OF THE WRITERS' WORKSHOPS

Most of the best books about fundraising are books about writing. That's good, because strong fundraising copy will raise more money than weak copy, all other things being equal.

All other things being equal is the problem, though. Because they aren't equal. Not even close. Several factors matter much more to the success of fundraising than the quality of the copy, such as:

- A great offer.
- A dialed-in audience.
- A strong brand presence.
- Low production costs.
- A well-balanced donor file.

Each of these things matters more than good writing. If you have any combination of them, you can raise funds successfully, even with mediocre to weak copy. And if you're badly lacking in those areas, even the best writing won't save the day.

All that emphasis on good writing gives a wrong impression: that the ultimate fundraising skill is writing, and that the greatest fundraiser is always a great writer. It encourages some people to neglect the other fundamentals. It also leads to a lot of seriously overwritten, show-offish fundraising copy. You can't be *too good*, right?

Nine-year-old Sophia was only halfway back home from the well, carrying a pot of water that weighed almost as much as she did. The tropical sun beat down on her face, and stinging sweat beads rolled into her eyes.

You get the picture: writing techniques taken straight from creative writing workshops.

The problem with that kind of writing is that it's not the way mentally healthy people talk. It's the way writers write.

(continued)

It's writing for art or entertainment. Not motivation. Writing that way in fundraising is like wearing a tuxedo to a burger joint.

A superb fundraising writer manages to have all the sensory details, emotion, rhythm, and all the other fireworks of superior writing. But it still sounds like a note dashed off by your friend. It's full of great technique, but the technique is barely visible.

On the whole, you're better off mastering a casual, colloquial, real-person voice than sounding like a novelist.

And if you really, truly want to have a lot of impact on fundraising, become a statistician.

REPORTING BACK: SET YOURSELF APART

The first thing you say to someone when he comes home at the end of the day is almost always something like "How was your day?"

Humans want feedback. We need to know how things are going. That's why we pay so much attention to report cards (our own or especially our kids'), performance reviews, and gossip. These things are deeply compelling, even when they tell us news we don't like.

If your donors give you money, but they never find out what happened with that money—you have created a disconnect. Almost a betrayal.

Donors need to know, too. If your donors give you money, but they *never find out what happened with that money*—you have created a disconnect. It's almost a betrayal. Imagine what your relationship with your significant other would be like if every day he or she came home and stonily refused to tell you about their day. It would be like living with a teenager!

■ 163 ■

A receipt can get donors part of the way there: It tells them the gift was received and the check was cashed. But they still need rich, emotional proof that the money accomplished something. They gave to make something happen; most receipts don't tell them that it happened. For all they know, maybe it didn't. They're stuck wondering: Did those hungry children who broke my heart get the food they needed? Did the research continue on its path of discovery? Is there going to be a ballet season next year?

And yet the charities come back again and again, asking for more help without ever showing donors they made a difference. That doesn't close the loop. You haven't said, "It worked! Your gift made possible the miracle we promised it would!"

Given this silence, it's surprising that donors give at all, much less give a second or third time. Would you?

I can't prove this, but I think this lack of feedback is one of the reasons for dismayingly low donor retention rates across our industry. I'll tell you this: Most of the organizations I work with excel at reporting back to their donors, and their donor retention numbers stand head and shoulders above the national benchmarks.

The two key ingredients to people's reporting back are receipts and newsletters. We'll look at the best way to do both of these, as well as some other ways to tell donors what their gifts mean.

Receipts that Do the Job

In a way, a receipt is the thing a donor "buys" when she gives. I know that's an odd way to think about it, but what else does she get? Except for the receipt, the rewards for giving are mostly intangible.

You worked hard and applied all your knowledge to craft an effective ask. (I hope you did, anyway.) And it worked! People gave! They now deserve to be thanked in ways that are as specific, clear, and emotional as the message that prompted the gift. The front line of accomplishing that is the receipt.

Your receipts should be human, warm, interesting, and rewarding. They should be overwhelmingly positive in every detail:

 It's specific about what the donor's gift made possible. It should have copy that shows you know not only *how much* she gave but *what she gave to accomplish*. If you asked her to help provide new curtains for the theater, don't thank her for supporting live theater in the community. Thank her for the curtains!

- It's grateful. You cannot overdo thankfulness.

 It doesn't use designation codes or cryptic phrases to indicate where the gift went. It uses plain language that matches what motivated the gift.

- It includes a letter or note from someone, signed by someone (preferably the person who asked in the first place or someone the donor has heard of).

- It includes pictures of what her gift did, if possible.

- If it's the donor's first gift to your organization, it should welcome her to the family.

And here's one of the most important qualities of a receipt: It's *quick!* If it takes you more than 48 hours to drop a paper receipt in the mail, you are being discourteous to your donors, and you're missing a key window for making them feel good about their gift. That means you are probably losing subsequent gifts.

Our donors live in a world of instant gratification. They can get almost anything they want *right now*. Nonprofits have largely failed to give this level of service. They often take days, weeks, or longer to acknowledge a donor's gift.

A slow receipt can cost you dearly. It's often a factor for those donors who give once and never again. Charitable giving produces a "warm glow"—a good feeling. It's part of what a donor wants when she gives. A quick receipt can prolong or reawaken the glow by arriving before it's forgotten. A receipt that takes too long to arrive misses the magic moment.

And it's just rude. A long-delayed gift sends a clear signal: *Your gift didn't really matter.*

Donor Newsletters

Your donors aren't exactly clamoring for you to send them more stuff. But when asked, they often mention that *they like newsletters.* It's one type of communication donors actually want from you. Even a lousy newsletter gives them some sense of what's happening with their money. It's a window into the organization—what's going on, how the cause is going, what's important.

But let's not settle for a weak newsletter.

Some nonprofit newsletters have almost nothing to do with donors. They are more often prolonged puff pieces about the organization. They're produced by, for, and about insiders. All the content is focused on how efficient, cutting-edge, famous, and cool the organization is.

A donor newsletter is about donors and *the impact of their giving.* It is a powerful tool for bonding with donors.

MORE TIPS FOR A STRONG DONOR NEWSLETTER

Here are five tips that can have immediate impact on your donor newsletter, improving donor engagement and most likely increasing the money they give in response.

1. *Tell wonderful stories.* This is the number-one duty of donor newsletters—to thrill your donors with stories that demonstrate the impact of their giving. Make the donor the hero of these stories: *This is possible because of your gifts!* When you do this consistently and well, you build the foundation of a lasting and satisfying relationship with your donors.

2. *Write amazing headlines.* Write 'em like the supermarket tabloids: big, bold, and built around muscular verbs.

(continued)

That's what the tabloids specialize in—the kind of headline that pulls readers into stories. They understand what we should also embrace: Your job is to entice people to read your newsletter.

3. *Write and design for skimmability and readability.* Short sentences. Short paragraphs. Lots of subheads, callouts, captions, and other attention-grabbing elements. Plenty of white space and images. Other than you and a few of your colleagues, nobody has to read your newsletter. It's up to you to earn their interest by making it easy and compelling.

4. *Ask for donations.* Even though the main purpose of your donor newsletter is to show them how their giving makes a difference, it's okay to ask, too. If you don't ask, you won't receive. Giving feels good, and asking doesn't insult donors. Don't wander from the main purpose of the newsletter, but go ahead and ask. And *always* include a reply coupon in your newsletter!

5. Never use that standard photo of a well-healed donor presenting a giant check (for a giant amount) to your organization's leaders. It emphasizes to your average donors that their checks are tiny and unimportant by comparison.

The Content

A donor-focused newsletter is packed with content that includes the donor as part of the story of success. Most of the stories are accounts of success, framed as accomplishments made possible by the donor. This is not difficult. Simply address the donor directly at key points of the story:

-   The headline: "Last Christmas, Bill lived under a bridge. This year, he's with his kids again, thanks to you."

- The lead (or somewhere early in the story): "Most people would have written Bill off. But you didn't. Thanks to your generosity, he has pulled his life back together."

- The conclusion: "Bill's transformation is a miracle. It's a miracle made possible by you. Your generous giving to the mission changed his life—and the lives of many others."

Each story should be a breathtaking account of something wonderful your organization did, not statistics about the accomplishments of an Awesome Nonprofit.

The writing style of a donor-focused newsletter should be well-told feature stories, not objective journalism. Chuck the inverted-pyramid structure and the studious avoidance of taking sides. The rules of newswriting don't apply here—you are a passionate advocate of your cause and the work your donors are funding. You are telling stories, not doing journalism.

Make your writing style major in these three qualities:

- *Informal.* It draws the reader in, directly making her part of the story, part of the cause, and part of your organization.

- *Dramatic.* It focuses on the things that make stories interesting: conflict, danger, courage, transformation, relationships.

- *Readable.* Short words, short sentences, short paragraphs. Many visual entry points to encourage reading.

Other Ways of Reporting Back

Great receipts and newsletters will do a lot to make donors realize how much they matter. But there's more you can do. Surprise donors with information about their impact. Lavish them with thanks and updates. Things like these:

Send special progress reports by mail or e-mail about ongoing projects they support. Think of these as reports to investors.

⭐ *Invite donors to phone conferences or webinars about the work.* Only a few will take you up on it, but inviting them can make donors feel important and appreciated. The asking is the thing.

⭐ *Thank donors by phone.* No ask, no other agenda. Just gratitude. (This is a proven retention booster.)

Reporting back is how you fight cynicism. You'll know it's working when you see better donor retention, more upgrading, and better word-of-mouth spreading through the marketplace about you.

DONOR CONTROL OVER COMMUNICATION

We don't control donors. They are in the driver's seat and can leave us at any time. And they do. There's nothing we can do to change that fact.

But we can work *with* their control.

Overtly give your donors the control they already have. Actively solicit their control, giving them choices like these:

- Let them choose the media you contact them with. Let them opt in or out of telephone, e-mail, or direct mail.

- Ask them what topics they'd prefer to hear from you about.

- Let them control how often you reach out to them.

- Let them leave your list if they want to.

✳ Do this by sending them (by mail and/or e-mail) questionaires that give them these choices. Here's what will happen: few donors will exercise any of these choices. But overall retention and other donor metrics will improve. That includes the large majority who don't opt for any of the choices you put in front of them.

Will you lose donors? A few. But you were going to lose those ones anyway—after you spent several dollars trying to get response that was never coming.

The real impact will be donors who trust you more, feel more connected, give more, and stay with you longer. It's one of the strongest fundraising techniques available to you.

APPROPRIATE DESIGN

Design can be a difficult subject for fundraisers. Most of us (myself included) are not graphic designers. We depend on professional designers to get our messages out in ways that won't embarrass us. It doesn't always work.

The right designer can take great fundraising ideas and breathe pure right-brain power into them. They can move your fundraising to levels of emotional resonance that words alone can hardly approach. The wrong designer—even a slightly wrong one—can turn your work into a pudding of awfulness that costs you dearly by confusing or even repelling donors.

One reason it's so hard to get design right is a false dichotomy held by many in the marketing and advertising industries: They think "creative" and "old-fashioned" are opposites. *Creative* means something brand new and exciting, that expresses the soul and genius of the designer. *Old-fashioned* means design that a designer is tired of. Effectiveness is seldom considered in this calculation.

Designers who are trapped in that mind-set will hurt your fundraising (and make your life miserable). Find designers who understand that creative and old-fashioned are not opposites. Find designers who know you can (and must) do both.

The opposite of boring design is not edgy, fad-driven modern design. The opposite of boring design is good *design. Readable, likable, and packed with the emotions of philanthropy.*

Don't get me wrong: Boring, bland, unemotional design hurts fundraising. Don't put up with it! But the opposite of boring design is not edgy, modern design, as some would have you believe. The opposite of boring design is *good* design. Readable, likable, and packed with the emotions of philanthropy. And it's usually old-fashioned.

This can be a challenge, because many designers are younger people, recently educated, conversant with high-tech tools. They've seen cutting-edge design receive all the praise, win the awards, and get covered by design publications. This gives them the false sense that looking up-to-the-minute is a high virtue. And that looking old-fashioned is a terrible sin. As we'll see in a moment, neither is true.

DESIGN TECHNIQUES FUNDRAISERS SHOULD ALMOST NEVER USE

Here are some design techniques you might be tempted to use because they *look good*. Don't. Each of these techniques seriously impedes readability. Whatever they give in attractiveness, you will more than lose in response.

Sans-Serif Fonts in Print Materials

Stick to serif fonts for text. Sans-serif fonts are measurably more difficult to read, and difficulty blocks engagement. Don't let this seemingly small detail be a barrier to your donors. (You can use sans-serif fonts for headlines or other large-type elements.)

The opposite is true for online text: Sans-serif fonts are easier to read on screens. (This may change as screen resolutions improve and move toward the same readability properties as paper.)

Reverse Type

Light type against dark background is almost completely unreadable. If you set any text this way, just assume it won't be read. This applies also to reverse type's evil cousin, type over images.

Some designers love these type treatments because they turn text into graphic elements. That's exactly what you should never do with text you want people to read.

Type over Tints

Type over any color other than white is hard to read. When the tint is light—10 percent or lighter—the negative impact starts

(continued)

to go away. Type over tint should be done rarely, and only over the lightest of tints.

Colored Type

We saw above that type should be set over a white background. That's not all. The type has to be black. That's right: Black text on a white background is almost the only way to go. (Large-type elements can be a color other than black, as long as it's a dark color.)

Here are the four main design qualities you should focus on:

- *Readability.* This is the most important design value in fundraising. If design impedes readability, it is a *failure.* No matter what else it has going for it. Please don't tolerate stupid design tricks like weird fonts, tiny type, or type set over images. These things squeeze the readability out of your copy. They make it opaque to donors, and that means less response.

- *Simple, not flashy.* I have yet to see a cool, stand-out piece of design outperform simple design in any fundraising medium. In fact, "undesigned" pieces[1] usually do best of all: text-only e-mails, direct-mail envelopes with no pictures or fancy type treatments. Flashy may be where it's at in some forms of marketing. Not in fundraising.

- *Culturally appropriate for your donors.* You know how old your donors are. Design for them. What may look corny and dated to you likely looks cool to them. You have no duty (and no business) dragging them into the era of modern design.

---

1. "Undesigned" messages require truly skilled and mature designers who can make it readable and emotive while leaving little trace of professional design.

(And you'll be in their shoes someday, longing for the look that resonates with you after young designers have moved on to newer things.)

- _Flexible._ Fundraising thrives on variety. A straightjacket design scheme that forces uniformity will drive down your fundraising results over time. That contradicts standard branding theory, but it's true. If you always design something a certain way, then you test that against something different (assuming both are appropriate), the new way will almost always perform better.

There's a lot more to design than these four things, but watch these four and you'll be in good shape.

HOW TO MEASURE DONOR COMMUNICATION

Fundraising is unkind to blowhards. The moment you pontificate, something comes along and proves you wrong. Believe me about this.

That means you should take everything any expert, consultant, or blowhard tells you with a grain of salt. That includes me. My advice to you is based on my experience, not yours. Things could be different for you.

Fortunately, there's an antidote for this lack of certainty: _measurement._

If you measure the right things, you'll know if the communications you're putting into practice are actually doing the job of connecting with donors so they give more and stay with you longer. The more you measure, the clearer your picture. Watch the following three indicators, and you'll have clarity:

1. _Campaign results._ If you're doing donor communication right, most of your fundraising campaigns will do well. Response, average gift, and net revenue are the key numbers to watch. When they are strong and in balance, you are seeing a healthy donor-focused program in action.

■ 173 ■

If you measure *only* campaign results, though, you could easily miss the real story. That's why the next two numbers are so important.

2. *Donor retention.*[2] This is a long-term metric, and it can uncover problems and opportunities not revealed by campaign results. Donors who feel connected and satisfied are much more likely to stay with you and keep giving. If you're communicating well with your donors, you should see strong (and usually rising) retention. These rates will differ by donor group (new donors have the lowest retention rates, and it improves with each year a donor stays with you).

   Even a small improvement in donor retention has a huge impact on your long-term revenue picture.

3. *Donor migration.* Every year, most donors give close to (usually exactly) the amount they gave the previous year. But some of them give more or less by a large percentage. Most significant upgrading and downgrading is a result of events in your donors' lives, and has little connection to what you are doing. But you do have influence: When your fundraising is striking a chord, you'll increase upgrading and minimize downgrading.

Donor retention is important because upgrading donors are your main (maybe only) source of major donors and eventual bequests. When you treat donors right, more of them will increase their giving, often because your relevant fundraising lifts you into the category of preferred charity for them.

These are not the only things you should be measuring, but they are the key indicators of successful donor-focused fundraising.

• • •

---

2. Expressed as the percentage of donors who give another gift in the year following the previous gift.

There's one more thing you should know about Golden Rule fund-raising: Even when you practice it and watch the revenue roll in as a result, it will likely come under attack.

Golden Rule fundraising doesn't stroke the egos of people in your organization. It's too busy making your donors into heroes, and that's not as thrilling as hyped-up boasting and organizational preening.

That's a common and unpleasant fact of life in our industry.

The reason is simple: Golden Rule fundraising doesn't stroke the egos of people in your organization. It's too busy making your donors into heroes, and that's not as thrilling as hyped-up boasting and organizational preening.

Even worse, Golden Rule fundraising is not a "shiny object." It's old hat. You don't need new technology. Just the right kind of attitude. Many leaders are irresistibly drawn toward new and exciting things and the amazing claims you can make for anything before it's been field-tested.

Being successful at fundraising should be satisfying enough, but that's a fact that's often lost on nonprofit leaders. Nearly every time I've seen organizations choose to abandon Golden Rule fundraising in favor of some form of Awesome Nonprofit fundraising, they did so with the claim that they could improve revenue by being cooler, more modern, more like commercial marketing.

It doesn't work. But try telling that to someone who has what he thinks is one solution for two problems: a spiffy new look-at-us approach that will *raise more money* and *make us feel good*.

I'm not trying to depress you—just to prepare you for what's coming. Your best move will be to marshal the facts about how being donor focused works financially. If you can't talk them out of Awesome Nonprofit fundraising, see if you can at least get them to test it first.

In the next two chapters, we'll look at some of the steps you can take to spread donor focus widely around your organization. That's the best way of all to fend off any attacks on your Golden Rule fundraising.

TAKEAWAYS FOR NONPROFIT BRAND BUILDERS

- Fundraising that motivates donors is centered around them, not the organization. Practice Golden Rule fundraising, not Awesome Nonprofit fundraising.
- The best stories for fundraising are ones where the donor is the hero.
- You can set yourself apart in donors' minds by promptly and thoroughly reporting back to them on the positive impact they've made by giving.
- Appropriate fundraising design is simple, readable, and usually old-fashioned.
- Donor-focused fundraising will be opposed in most organizations.

To do:

① Send out questionnaire w/ communication options.

② See if I can figure out our retention rate.

CHAPTER THIRTEEN

The Structure of a Donor-Focused Nonprofit

> The truly successful nonprofit brands are those that build their love and respect for donors into their structure. Here are some of the things that work to put donors at the center of your work.

When your interpreter is weeping too much to tell you what was just said, you know you're being told a sad story.

Only people who work in fundraising have experiences like this: I interviewed a caregiver at an orphanage in Omsk, a run-down Detroit of a city in Siberia. (Dostoevsky was sent there as a punishment for revolutionary activity, which tells you something about the place.) The caregiver had brought a little boy named Kirill (pronounced *Key-REAL*) because she wanted me to know his story.

Kirill was asleep on my lap, as limp as a ribbon of seaweed.

The Soviet Union collapsed a few weeks after my visit. While I was there, the once inescapable apparatus of the Soviet State was going up in smoke. It left breathtaking new freedoms, but also rising poverty, lawlessness, decay, and alcoholism. There was widespread fear that the coming winter would bring a famine and starve millions.

The orphanage was ill-lit and dirty. Clearly, it had never been a pleasant or child-friendly place. But as the State and the Communist Party crumbled, the structures that supported places like orphanages dissolved, too. The workers were struggling to feed and care for the swelling population of children without parents—many of them handicapped or otherwise in need of special care.

Like Kirill. His mother was an "incorrigible alcoholic," one of those staggering drunks you saw everywhere in Soviet cities. She'd left him on a park bench one icy day a couple of years before, when he was too small to follow her. Now Kirill was six years old—the age of my own son at the time—though he looked more like he was four. He was thin, with translucent skin and wispy blond hair that seemed permanently charged with static. He moved slowly, like someone underwater.

I've been to understaffed orphanages around the world. The children in these places seldom see men. They're afraid, yet they hunger for attention. Kirill did what kids in those places usually do: At first he cowered behind the caregiver, flinching when he heard my voice. After a few minutes he worked his way closer until he was leaning against me, almost like a cat. Suddenly, he went limp. He'd gone to sleep standing there. I lifted him onto my lap to keep him from falling.

He's weak—not healthy, the caregiver said through the intepreter. *He falls asleep like that. He gets nosebleeds. He can't yet speak. We don't have a doctor to examine him.*

I put my hand on his forehead. It was clammy and hot, the way my kids feel when they're sick. That feeling triggers a reflex in a parent: *Do something.* All I could do was hear, and then tell, his story.

When you conduct an interview through a translator, you get the information in flat, factual packets. Facial expressions and other emotional cues happen before you know what they're about. The caregiver's voice became more quiet. She shook her head and looked at the floor. *Kirill shows signs of brain damage. From his mother's drinking. Possibly made worse by malnutrition.*

She hid her face in her hands: *None of the children eat well. All we can give them is borscht. No protein. There are so many of them, and only food we can beg from neighbors.*

When they found Kirill in the park, he was hypothermic, his lips blue, ice in his hair. *He has not recovered from that. He is never well. The children call him Snowman.*

That's when my interpreter started weeping. Then sobbing. She couldn't catch her breath and kept trying to apologize to me and to the caregiver. Kirill slept, breathing lightly.

Decades later, I still think about Kirill. Did things at the orphanage improve? How serious was his cognitive damage? Could he ever function on his own? He'd be a young adult by now. What kind of a man is he?

When you see things breaking apart, you realize that structure matters. Who's responsible for what. Where the money comes from and goes. A broken structure breaks a lot of other things. Like it did for a little Russian boy named Kirill.

Your structure matters, too. It may not be a matter of life and death (though in some cases it might), but the way you structure your organization has a deep impact on your ability to raise funds and keep your mission going.

A lot of what it takes to structure a nonprofit is common sense, no different from any other type of organization: Consistency. Balance. Trust. Clarity of purpose and roles. Policies that serve people.

CHARACTERISTICS OF A WELL-RUN NONPROFIT

- Aligned around fundraising goals.
- Not run by committees.
- No marketing department.
- Plan for every donor.
- Good data.
- Donor connected.

Beyond those things, here are some structural characteristics of well-run nonprofits that excel in fundraising. Adjusting your organization to these can help you build a better, more effective brand.

A WELL-RUN NONPROFIT IS ALIGNED AROUND FUNDRAISING GOALS

I'm only an amateur musician, so what I have to say isn't all that important. But I have to get this off my chest.

I play the string bass. (That's the big one.) It's designed to make low notes. Those of us who play are trained to make low notes on it. It's not where the glory and drama of the music happen, but it would be a lot less glorious and dramatic without us.

Sometimes, in orchestral music, bassists have to play higher notes. They're still low, just high for the instrument. These higher notes force us to use "thumb position." Instead of holding down the strings with the tips of the four fingers on your left hand, you also use the outside of your thumb, pressing down with the area between the nail and the knuckle (see Exhibit 13.1).

If that makes you wince, I've succeeded in capturing the essence of thumb position. Because it hurts. It really hurts.

I don't have the capacity any more for that pain. I've decided not to play any more high notes in thumb position. Sorry, Mozart. Sorry,

EXHIBIT 13.1

This is thumb position. It hurts.

Brahms. I know you want those notes, but they don't work with my priorities or tolerance for pain. I'm finished with thumb position.

Okay, not really. Every musician knows that a certain amount of pain is part of the deal. I'd never get away with a no-thumb-position policy. But some nonprofits tolerate people taking I-do-it-my-way positions like that.

On any fundraising team there are people whose function is indirectly connected with asking and receiving: the people who keep the computers running, the people who pay the bills, the office managers, human resources—you might think of them as the "bass players" of the team.

Their jobs put them a step or two away from the fundraising action. They may not feel as important as frontline fundraisers, but they are. And when they don't share the same fundraising priorities, they can create real problems. . . .

You've met the IT manager who believes his job is to make the network run to his specifications with as little hassle to him as possible, even when that means it doesn't do what everyone else needs it to do. Or the person in accounting who makes it hard to get anything done in her quest to make things go smoothly for her?

I've known organizations that couldn't acknowledge gifts in anything like a timely manner. That was the job of an operations department, and it would be "too disruptive" for people's schedules.

I also know a startling number of otherwise excellent organizations that have dysfunctional giving pages on their web site. The people who run the web site don't want to deal with the technical complexities of getting it right for donors. Online giving is the fastest-growing part of fundraising. But not for those organizations. Their webmasters figure the loss of a few online gifts is not that important, not worth their trouble.

They think and act in these ways that seem dysfunctional, because *it makes sense for them*. They are accomplishing the narrow goals that are placed before them. The fact that they're impeding the *real goal* of raising funds is beside the point—their point. If fundraising goals aren't met, what's the loss?

(I hasten to add that I've encountered many nonprofit support staff who routinely go far beyond the call of duty to make fundraising work. True heroes and models for us all.)

If your organization depends on money from fundraising, everyone should have their success, including their compensation, tied to fundraising success. Even if their role in that success may be indirect, it's still critical.

If your organization needs money from fundraising, everyone should have their success, including their compensation, tied to fundraising success.

If fundraising is going poorly, it's everyone's "fault." It should be more difficult for anyone to get increased rewards or promotions than when fundraising is going well. It needs to be clear that everyone rises or sinks together with their common enterprise of raising funds. Don't ignore the problem or write it off to environmental factors you can't control. People in other professional sectors don't get to do that.

Along with that should be a de-siloing of functions: The managers and leaders of all the groups need to be working together, not in isolation. They all have to be able to see the problems of others as their own problems, too.

This won't be easy if your organization has been operating in separate silos. It's important, though. Getting it right can unleash energy, focus, and innovation in your organization.

A WELL-RUN NONPROFIT IS NOT RUN BY COMMITTEES

You'll be surprised to hear me say this, but there's a force at work in many nonprofits that's *worse for fundraising than Brand Experts: committees*. They do more harm, and they are even more common.

Committees are meant to bring together expertise. They don't. Instead, they *pool incompetence*. That's the inevitable outcome of a group in which everyone is functionally equal and encouraged to speak. Each member's opinion gets full hearing, whether they know what they're talking about or not.

Here's what happens when a committee gets hold of a quality best-practices fundraising appeal:

- There's someone who says, "Too much copy. No one will read it."

- There's always a smart person who says, "Too emotional. People won't respond. Make it more intellectual."

- Then there's an educated person who says, "Don't talk down to the donors. They'll be insulted."

- There's at least one "formalizer." You know the type: Short words like "gift" become long words like "donation," and colloquial words like "kids" become formal words like "children." And you must not start a sentence with a conjunction. And you can't use contractions. Or use sentence fragments. Ever.

- There's usually a brand defender whose straitjacket interpretation of brand standards does not include any fundraising best practices.

- There's someone who's afraid of change.

- And someone else who's allergic to anything that's been done before.

All that adds up to a lot of costly bad advice. It should be ignored. But it can't, because it comes with the authority of the committee.

Everyone knows committees are a terrible way to produce good work. Yet committees live on, doing uncalculated damage every day.

Here's my challenge to you: Make your organization one of the few, one of the proud, that dispatches with committees and reaps the rewards of better fundraising. All that's stopping you are inertia and the expectations of a few people who enjoy committee work.

The good news is that most people are thrilled to be freed from a committee. They have jobs to do, and sitting around opining about things they don't understand is not their idea of a great time. (The people who want to be on a committee are the ones you'd probably be better off without.)

Here's how to get the work done instead:

Replace each committee with two or three people who have *specific* and *relevant* expertise. Limit their authority to their areas of competence. Make sure these people are held responsible for fundraising results. That will keep them focused and realistic.

Your balance sheet will thank you.

A WELL-RUN NONPROFIT DOESN'T HAVE A MARKETING DEPARTMENT

Do you have a marketing department? Quick—fire it! Your brand will be healthier and your fundraising more successful without a marketing department because *a marketing department is the wrong tool for a fundraising organization.*

Note that I didn't say, "Marketing is the wrong tool." In fact, marketing is a critical tool for any nonprofit that intends to build a brand, raise funds, and grow. But when marketing is the responsibility of a department, it almost always leads you down expensive blind alleys that don't lead to improved results.

WHY MARKETING MATTERS FOR FUNDRAISING

Marketing can lead you astray when it's unconnected to fundraising. But fundraising in a vacuum can be just as harmful.

Here's how it can go wrong: If you rigorously follow direct-response testing results with no guidance from the marketing and branding disciplines, your organization eventually will become indistinct from others with similar missions.

(continued)

Your message will become a reflection of your target donors and their preferences. You'll maximize an ever-narrower segment of donors until growth outside that box becomes nearly impossible.

Marketing is about differentiation. Being distinct from others. Fundraising is about effectiveness—with or without differentiation. Often, what works for one organization also works for a similar organization. This can lead the two organizations to becoming alike. That's why fundraisers need marketing in their toolbox.

Well-executed marketing injects differentiation and uniqueness into the equation. That's what can keep your message from spiraling into smaller and smaller hyperefficient circles.

Yes, we need marketing.

Who brings home the bacon in your organization? Probably your fundraising department. Fundraisers are good at raising funds. That's because they're held accountable to measurable financial goals. They become adept at maximizing and refining their work in pursuit of those goals.

The outcomes of marketing are tougher to quantify, especially when they aren't directly connected to fundraising goals. Many marketing departments don't even try to measure their impact. Those who do measure tend to pursue qualitative goals like "mindshare" and "awareness."

It doesn't matter how much mathematical rigor you apply to qualitative measurement. It all adds up to nothing you can take to the bank. You could spend literally millions of dollars to nudge your awareness index upward—and have no impact on the bottom line, other than the expense.

That's exactly what many nonprofit marketing departments do: spend a lot of money, get nothing in return, and obscure the situation with reports and presentations that keep implying that a pot of gold is just around the corner.

It isn't. There is no pot of gold.

Wasted money is only part of the problem. Marketing departments and fundraising departments have such fundamentally different goals, they almost always end up with two parallel or even conflicting messaging platforms:

- Fundraising, which is literal, action oriented, and donor focused.

- Marketing, which in many cases is conceptual and inward focused.

These two messaging strategies are so unlike each other that many nonprofits just hope the same audience will never encounter both. It's not just that one message fails to support the other; they are in direct conflict.

Nonprofit marketing people have told me, without a hint of irony, "Our fundraising is effective at raising revenue, but it's damaging the brand."

Nonprofit marketing people have told me, without a hint of irony, "Our fundraising is effective at raising revenue, but it's damaging the brand." In that mind-set, the organization's "brand" is a thing separate from fundraising. The organization is forced to choose between correctly expressing the brand and raising money! That's like the old medical punch line: "The operation was a success, but the patient died." We got the brand nailed—but we didn't raise any money.

"Brand" can and should exist to *improve* fundraising. If it doesn't, it's a failure. Too many marketing departments don't accept that.

But beyond that, the very existence of a marketing department lets everyone else in the organization off the hook. They can accurately say about marketing, "That's not my department."

Marketing is too important to leave up to marketers. If marketing isn't built into your entire organization from top to bottom and side to side, you will always struggle to tell your story and be interesting to potential donors.

It's *everyone's job* to tell the story of your cause in a way that will help others choose to get involved. It's *everyone's job* to create memorable, exciting programs that outsiders can support. It's *everyone's job* to take part in the conversation about your cause. It's *everyone's job* to know, understand, and respect donors.

I'm not proposing some kind of hippy-dippy future, where program directors are writing direct mail and accountants are designing web sites. We'll always need the specific skills of good fundraising and marketing: copy, design, strategy, plus media and production expertise. If you want that stuff done right, you need professionals to do their jobs.

But when the marketing department takes responsibility for marketing and nobody else does, it will fail. A stand-alone marketing department simply can't stand alone.

Worse yet, if you leave marketing to marketers, they'll fall short, not only because they aren't sufficient to the task—they'll also fail because they'll do it wrong. You see, locked away in their own department, they'll come to view themselves as gatekeepers for all marketing functions. They'll spend their time (and your money) controlling the message and shushing everyone else.

They'll be the ones who hire Brand Experts.

Meanwhile, their eyes on the wrong prize, they'll neglect the real job of marketing: building a truly remarkable organization, taking part in the genuine conversation that forms around such organizations, and finding partners who care enough to support it.

Maybe back in the "Mad Men" days, marketing used to be about fonts, color palettes, and tightly defined messaging platforms. These days of empowered customers and free-flowing information, it's about conversation, action, collaboration, and authenticity. Complex stuff. Hard to understand. Harder to put into practice. And nearly impossible if you have an isolated, out-of-context marketing department.

So if you have a marketing department, get rid of it.

But think twice before you get rid of the marketing people. Once they're aligned with measurable revenue goals, you may find them invaluable. Unless they're recalcitrant and unable to work with the well-defined and hypermeasured world of fundraising, you'll do well to repurpose and integrate them.

HOW TO DEAL WITH DONOR COMPLAINTS

Having a donor-focused fundraising program doesn't mean you never get complaints from donors. In fact, complaints often signal that you're doing something right. If you're grabbing people by the collar and getting their attention, you'll make some donors uncomfortable—and some of them will complain. Get used to it.

Many complainers are loyal donors who are experiencing something that doesn't work for them. They're going to the trouble of making it right. You can—and should—satisfy them, or at least try to. (Some complainers are just bellyachers. You'll never make *them* happy.)

When you deal with a complainer, *be thankful*. This person is giving you a chance to serve her better and turn a negative feeling into a positive experience. Find out exactly what she wants—and do it.

Here are three common donor complaints and how you can turn a complaint into a positive connection.

- *Complaint:* You send too much mail.
    - *Positive response:* We track everything we send to make sure we're spending our money wisely. We know you can't give in response to every message you receive. Give when it's the right thing for you to do. If we're sending more mail than you want, that's not the best use of our money. We'd be happy to reduce the amount of mail we send you.

(continued)

■ 188 ■

- *Complaint:* You're wasting money.
  - *Positive response:* Every dollar we spend on our mailings results in several dollars coming back. We watch this closely, and we've been able to keep our expenses low compared to the amount of money people give us. If we're sending too much to you, then that's a waste, and we don't want to do it.
- *Complaint:* You're giving me a guilt trip.
  - *Positive response:* It's not our intent to make you feel guilty. Please accept our apology. We pay close attention to what we say and the way we say it. We communicate with a lot of urgency because the need for what we do is so great. Would you like us to avoid sending you this type of message?

The truth works (almost) every time. For complaints about anything from telemarketing to the colors you use, the answer is this: What we're doing works, but we're happy to let you opt out of it.

A WELL-RUN NONPROFIT HAS A PLAN FOR EVERY DONOR

Quiz: Which of the following types of donors most often "fall between the cracks" in fundraising programs and end up being ignored by the organization?

A. Lapsed donors
B. Under $5 donors
C. High-end donors
D. Foreign currency donors

It's C. It happens again and again. The loss of revenue is staggering.

Most organizations know what to do with their top donors. They also know how to handle their general donors. The rules are clear and the procedures are followed.

But donors in the middle—between high and low, especially those at the upper end of the middle—are a conundrum for some nonprofits. They have a sense that these donors should be treated differently (which is correct). But how? Maybe they should get a higher, more appropriate form of communication (partly correct). So they are removed from the normal mail and e-mail program (big mistake).

It's hoped that major gift officers will take over with these donors and do their relational magic with them. But any major gift officer who's proprerly deployed doesn't have the bandwidth to take them on.

So these almost-top donors no longer get the fundraising that helped them rise to their present high value. They also don't get personal attention that in theory should pick up the baton and raise their giving level. It's as if they no longer exist. Or, to put it more accurately, it's like the organization no longer exists.

Months go by with no contact. The revenue from these important donors disappears. Then they lapse. Instead of around 20 percent of them lapsing in a year, as one might expect, 90 percent of them lapse. And once they're lapsed, most will never come back. Even if you work hard to entice them. They move on to other things.

The loss, depending on the size of the group, can easily be hundreds of thousands or even millions of dollars every year, for years to come. It would be better if your headquarters burned to the ground. At least you'd have insurance.

It should be impossible for this to happen.

It *will* be impossible if you have a plan for every donor at every giving level and every stage of their life cycle.

The plan needs to have an appropriate treatment for every donor group:

- When and how they'll be contacted.
- How much you can spend on them.

- What the messages and offers will be.
- What to do with donors who upgrade or downgrade.
- How to handle lapsed donors.
- How to handle new donors.

Your donor plan should be in writing, so when someone with institutional memory leaves, the knowledge stays intact, and no group is lost in the transition.

And it must be followed religiously. It can't be changed on a whim—only by new information that shows you a better way to treat a specific group.

A WELL-RUN NONPROFIT HAS ITS DONOR DATA ACT TOGETHER

There are a lot of books about how to write good fundraising copy. There's almost nothing about proper handling and use of donor data.

If you write weak, uncompelling fundraising copy, the damage is temporary. If you screw up your donor data, you can sink the ship.

That's unfortunate: If you write weak, uncompelling fundraising copy, the damage is temporary. And minor. If you screw up your donor data, you can sink the ship.

If your data are inaccurate, or you're not able to query it, or definitions are not consistent or documented, all kinds of bad things happen:

- You won't be in control of which donors you're communicating with.
- You may not even know for sure who's getting what.
- You can't tell what's working.
- You can't mail smarter (or not mail those you shouldn't mail).

And if you lose control of your data, you can *really annoy* donors. It's the one way nonprofits can torment our donors the way some poorly run companies do their customers.

Information matters. In a sense, it's all you have to offer. Don't let data problems fester. Instead, get the most detail-obsessed, anal-retentive person you've ever known in charge of donor data. Make sure you have an appropriate database system that fits your needs and the size of your donor file. Then protect it like it's your very life. Because that's what it is.

A WELL-RUN NONPROFIT IS DONOR CONNECTED

I once interviewed an agriculture expert working to help a cluster of rural communities in Africa improve food production. Her project involved building a lot of infrastructure (everything from storage sheds to a bridge over a nearby river), persuading people to embrace new and unfamiliar foods, even getting a couple of rival tribes to cooperate for the first time in their long history. The project eventually transformed life for hundreds of thousands of people.

Toward the end of the interview, she told me that when she joined the organization, she'd been offered a competitive salary but refused it. She believed in a different way of getting paid. She came out of an American Protestant tradition where "missionaries" (including agriculture professionals) raise their own support. They put together an ad hoc community of friends, family, and church members who give monthly to fund their work. That's what she'd done years ago and kept it going throughout her career.

As you know, raising (and keeping) your donors is no small task, especially for someone who has another job of a different type. I asked her why she wouldn't take the offer to walk away from the workload and stress of raising her own support. She knew exactly why, and she ticked off the reasons on her fingers:

- She didn't want to leave her supporters out of the work she was doing. They'd come to care deeply about the issues she worked on. Going onto salary would have meant her donors would lose contact with something that mattered to them.

- She didn't want to lose touch with the donors who had become like an extended family. She looked forward to writing her monthly letters to them. She loved hearing from them about their lives and concerns. They gave her perspective, and the connection was especially important for her in times of stress and loneliness.

- She wanted the extra nonmonetary support her donors provided: connection, encouragement, advocacy, and prayer. People who are giving money also give other things.

"Raising my support makes me a better agriculture specialist," she said. Then she smiled. "It makes my donors better people, too. That's as much my ministry as all this farming stuff."

A lot of good magic flows from being connected with donors. You need that magic all over your organization.

Raising your own support isn't for everyone. But meaningful contact with donors should be. At the least, everyone should spend time manning the phones to take calls from donors, making thank-you calls to donors (these calls can significantly boost subsequent giving), or writing thank-you notes to donors.

Contact with donors helps your staff understand that donors are *real people*. They meet them, know them, and get an understanding of who they really are, how they think, what they care about, and what they understand.

If you personally know a lot of donors (and not just those who are your friends anyway), it'll be harder to maintain unrealistic theories about how they should think. When donors frustrate you because they don't behave as you would (a frequent fact of life in our business), you'll have sympathy and understanding—not sputtering annoyance.

When Brand Experts unveil their work, you'll be able to spot any donor-irrelevant ideas immediately. Most of all, donor contact makes it easier to love them. And that's how fundraising is done—with love.

TAKEAWAYS FOR NONPROFIT BRAND BUILDERS

A well-run nonprofit that's focused on donors and raises a lot of funds:

- Is aligned around fundraising goals. Everyone is responsible for success in fundraising.
- Is not run by committees. People work in their areas of expertise.
- Has no marketing department. But lots of marketing!
- Has a plan for every donor. No matter what life stage or giving level.
- Has its data act together.
- Is donor connected. Everyone has some contact with donors.

CHAPTER FOURTEEN

The Culture of the Donor-Focused Organization

> Nonprofits that achieve the best fundraising results are those that are focused on their donors, see their donors as heroes, and learn to think like their donors.

One of my favorite things about baseball is how the players watch the game. When they aren't on the field, they line up along the fence between the dugout and the field. They lean over it like a row of 10-year-old boys, chewing gum, even elbowing each other like happy kids at a game.

I get a "morning in America" feeling when I see that: The game proceeds at its stately pace, the grass is green, the hot dogs savory, and the players are aligned with their fans, enjoying the game with the same sense of joy. All is well.

But my outlook darkens when I notice some of the players who aren't watching. There are always a few—usually the overpaid, underperforming superstars who seem to exist to drain the teams' budgets and make the fans stop caring. Those guys sit glumly on the bench, enduring the game, clearly signaling that they have something better to do. You almost can't blame them: After all, each season has 162 games, plus 30-some spring training games, plus (if they're lucky) playoff games. That's an awful lot of baseball.

But come on! This is *Major League Baseball!* They're living the dream. And they make a ton of money doing it.

If a handful of those disengaged baseball players is bad, imagine a whole team of them: players who find baseball an embarrassing exercise they only do so they can make their inflated salaries. They sit around and complain: about the rules of the game and the oafish fans who put them through the whole degrading spectacle. They imagine a better grade of fans—ones who will pay them without making them play the stupid game.

Those teams would always lose, no matter how talented the players. Baseball itself would disappear like a guttering candle flame if teams were like that. (Perhaps the greedy sourpusses scattered around the league are part of the reason the sport is past its glory days.)

Baseball isn't the only profession that harbors people who hate their work. I suppose you meet them everywhere, but I'm sad to say I see them all the time in fundraising.

You've met them, too—those unhappy, wish-there-were-another-way fundraisers who feel victimized by the demands of fundraising. They're always looking for better (usually younger) donors. They waste a lot of time and energy not raising funds because they constantly walk away from what works and flirt with anything that doesn't seem to them like fundraising. That's why they're easily taken in by Brand Experts.

Teams made up of fundraisers who love fundraising raise dramatically more money than those who wish they could find another way.

Fortunately, there's also another type of fundraiser: the thrilled-to-be-here, aligned-with-donors type who love the beauty of the fundraising house and are nerdily thrilled about motivating people to give. (I'm talking about *you*—the kind who's reading this book.) They make the fundraising world go 'round.

Teams made up of fundraisers who love fundraising raise dramatically more money than those who wish they could find another way. Aligned fundraisers love asking for money. They know donors love giving and are enriched by the transaction. They're excited about direct mail (and other old-line media) because they see the evidence every day that those high-touch connections touch donors' hearts and stir them to action.

They aren't looking for a magical brand formula or some amazing new social marketing phenomenon to rescue them from the day-to-day work of raising funds. They understand: They're already tapping into the magic.

They love their elderly donors. They see them as sources of wisdom and teachers of generosity—not as old-fashioned intransigents who ignore their big ideas and spoil their fun.

Shiny new objects and Next Big Things that sweep through the profession with a lot of sound and fury but have nothing to do with donors don't interest donor-aligned fundraisers. They want real innovations that make giving easier and more compelling for donors.

When your fundraising team is full of people who love fundraising you are in good shape. There will be more good ideas and fewer bad ones. Their joy spreads around the team and out to donors, who respond more and feel more connected. It's like the difference between an army that knows it's fighting for a just cause and one that's been force-marched to the battle for the benefit of its masters.

If my claims here strike you as far-fetched, look into your own mind: Think about the times you've had assignments that were thrilling and full of possibility. Now think about the half-baked, ill-conceived assignments that have dropped onto your desk. In which situation were you smarter, more creative, more inspired, and more likely to break through?

The difference between good and lousy assignments exists as much in your head as in the assignments themselves. You might have been completely wrong about the quality of the assignment. That doesn't matter. How you felt about it is what made the difference in your performance. That's how it is in fundraising.

If you love it, you're on your way to being brilliant. If you think it's a necessary evil, you hardly stand a chance.

ONE OF THE MOST IMPORTANT TRUTHS IN FUNDRAISING

If you believe your fundraising annoys donors, *you are right.*

Just as people who believe they're stupid are more prone to doing stupid things, you create your own fundraising reality. Your unhappy approach will leak out and make donors unhappy.

If you believe your fundraising is a welcome blessing in the lives of your donors—you'll create fundraising that's just that.

Attitude is everything.

No organization should tolerate antifundraising fundraisers. They are corrosive, and they hurt the cause. The biggest favor you can do them is let them go—free them from fundraising so they can find something that nourishes them. And free your organization from their negative influence.

A state of alignment with donors is one of the most important qualities of a donor-focused organization. It's the secret weapon of a money-raising nonprofit brand.

A state of alignment with donors is one of the most important qualities of a donor-focused organization. It's the secret weapon of a money-raising nonprofit brand. Nurturing and building a culture that encourages alignment should be among your most important goals. Remember Amalgamated Air in Chapter 2? If you harbor colleagues who hate fundraising, you are the nonprofit equivalent of that terrible company.

CHARACTERISTICS OF A DONOR-FOCUSED NONPROFIT

- It's investment-oriented.
- It has a fact-based culture.
- It doesn't treat all donors the same.
- It has a culture of thankfulness.
- Fundraising is part of its mission.

Let's look at some of the other ways to make your organization effective through your culture.

A DONOR-FOCUSED NONPROFIT IS INVESTMENT ORIENTED

When corporations fail to invest in their future, we shake our heads and wonder why they're so shortsighted. Like the once-important ice-delivery companies. They never grasped the value of home refrigerators, so they were destroyed by the new technology. How could they have been so shortsighted?

We should look at nonprofits the same way. Those that don't invest have a grim future ahead. Changing technology, demographics, media use, and competition will chip away at their fundraising revenue until the ground drops out from under them like a sinkhole.

The difference between an investment-oriented nonprofit and one that's not can be hard to see. To show you that difference, I'm going to plunge deep into the weeds for a moment. . . .

There are two key performance indicators in fundraising that measure exactly the same thing: return on investment (ROI) and cost per dollar raised (CPDR):

- *ROI* is revenue divided by cost: If you raised $600 from a campaign that cost $200, the ROI is 3. If you raised less than you spent, your ROI would be below 1. It is sometimes expressed as a ratio (3:1), a dollar amount ($3), or just as a number.

- *CPDR* goes the other way: cost divided by revenue. The preceding scenario, where it cost $200 to raise $600, would give a CPDR of $0.33—it cost 33 cents to raise each dollar. If you spent more than you raised, the CPDR would be above $1. CPDR is usually expressed as a dollar amount.

Both figures measure fundraising efficiency. They both answer, with some precision: *Was that worth it?* The actions for improving both ROI and CPDR are the same: You can lower costs and/or you can improve response. Responsible organizations pay attention to both.

I've encountered few organizations that use both ROI and CPDR. It's one or the other. And there's an important difference between the two types of organizations:

- ROI organizations tend to focus on *improving results*—that is, making their ROI higher. They make bolder decisions, innovate more often, and generally have a mind-set that they can and should make their fundraising better all the time. They are more investment-minded.

- CPDR organizations zero in on lowering their CPDR by cutting costs. This fosters a narrow approach and a fear of failure. Vision and innovation come hard and rarely for CPDR organizations. But hey, at least they keep costs down![1]

Which approach do you think is more likely to wow donors, win enthusiastic support, and uncover new ways to raise funds? Not the organization that's always looking for ways to *do less*. As everyone says, *You can't cut your way to greatness.*

Does measuring ROI instead of CPDR make you bolder? Or does having an investment mind-set lead you to prefer ROI? Chicken or egg? The important thing is that you should focus your thinking and planning on *investments*, on *opportunities*, on *improvement*.

---

1. I'll bet this is not exactly what you hope your tombstone will say.

An organization with an investment approach is always asking these questions:

- How will we reach donors we haven't reached before?
- How can we touch donors more deeply?
- What do our donors really want from us, and how can we give it to them?

They ask these questions, and they seek the answers. They spend time and money seeking them. They find partners that help them invest and think about the future. Of course, you owe your donors and your cause prudent frugality. But be sure to spend your best time and energy *investing in donors.*

WHAT TO TELL YOUR DONORS ABOUT OVERHEAD

For a long time, for too long, charity watchdogs and their friends in the media have kept a steady chorus of advice for donors: *The only smart way to give to charity is to give to organizations that have the lowest possible overhead.*

This "overhead is waste" mind-set has guaranteed limited growth (or no growth) for many nonprofits. Their need to keep overhead down has meant little innovation, not enough spending on donor acquisition to fuel growth, and reliance on ineffective staff—because they can't pay competitive salaries.

Recently, there's been a much-needed backlash against anti-overhead nonsense. It's being said out loud that overhead is not only necessary but good. It's investment.

Now that the issue is more in the open, how do we talk to donors about overhead?

The same way we did before.

If you have good watchdog ratings, *trumpet them.* Even if you understand their criteria to be incomplete or bogus. If you

(continued)

have low overhead, *brag about it*. Make sure donors see that old pie chart.

Many donors care about those things. Maybe they shouldn't, but they do.

If you don't have amazingly low overhead and/or you don't have maximum watchdog ratings—just don't talk about it. Make your case that the donor can make a difference by giving to you.

The overhead discussion is important, but we have no business using fundraising as a platform to persuade donors to change their minds. That would be irresponsible.

Your direct mail or e-mail is not going to change donors' attitudes about nonprofit overhead. Using direct mail to educate the public on a complex issue like this is like using an eggbeater to prevent plane crashes. It's not only the wrong tool, it's the wrong type of tool.

If you use your fundraising as a platform to fight the overhead misconception, you will raise less money for your cause. And that's dereliction of duty for a fundraiser. Any time a fundraising campaign tries to raise funds *plus* do something else—it hurts response, often dramatically. Every time.

Not only that, but it won't change anybody's attitude. You won't help improve the situation by changing minds. You might even make it worse by raising issues that weren't there in the first place.

Fight the overhead fight as a citizen. Not with your fundraising.

A DONOR-FOCUSED NONPROFIT HAS A FACT-BASED CULTURE

Do you like getting calls from telemarketers during dinner?

Neither do I. I haven't met many folks who say *I love it when my green beans congeal on my plate while a stranger who talks too fast tries to make me hate my phone/cable/data provider.*

But no matter how much you and I and all our friends hate telemarketing, our dislike does not prove that telemarketing is an ineffective medium. The only fact contained in the way we feel about telemarketing is that *we feel that way*. It reveals nothing about the quality of telemarketing, and it's not a fact about how other people will respond to it. (Really, it's not even a fact about how *we* will respond; it only reveals what we're willing to say out loud about it.)

You may find this hard to believe, but a meaningfully wide slice of the Great American Pie *loves* getting calls from telemarketers. They respond happily. Even more people say they don't care for the idea of telemarketing, but respond to the calls they get. It's like the way everybody hates the U.S. Congress, but most people like their own representative.

If you don't use telemarketing in your fundraising because you (or your leaders) personally dislike telemarketing—you are not basing your decision on facts. You're making a classic intellectual error: *I hate it, so everybody else must hate it, too.* Most people grow out of that error between the ages of 5 and 17. But for some reason it hangs on in nonprofit decision making.

It's the same if you base a decision on your *likes*. What would you think of someone who said, "I love MySpace! We should be investing heavily there!" That's exactly what you do when you make any decision based on your personal connection with it.

Professional fundraisers develop a mental habit of separating their own tastes and preferences from their knowledge of what does and doesn't work.

Professional fundraisers develop a mental habit of separating their own tastes and preferences from their knowledge of what works. That's a career-long process, but I'll give you the first and most dependable fact about your likes compared to what motivates your donors:

If you like it, donors are not likely to respond.

That's the smart working assumption in fundraising. Your likes and dislikes tend to run opposite to donor response. This inverse correlation isn't total, so you still have to get the facts.[2] But it's so frequent that it's where you should start.

It's possible your donors will hate telemarketing as much as you do. It might turn out to be a poor channel for reaching them. Possible, but not likely. There's one way to know: try it. As long as you rely on your intuition about it, you are more likely wrong than right.

A fact-based approach will make you more effective. Your thinking will be clearer. You'll spend less time pursuing half-baked ideas that don't stand a chance. Your decisions—the big ones about strategy down to the small ones about word choice—will turn out better more often. You'll be far less susceptible to snake-oil con artists hawking things like faddish new Web portals, and you'll be able to discern the good from the bad when you talk to Brand Experts.

As a fact-based fundraiser, you'll be better equipped to make a dozen decisions a day. Let me give you a small head start in three areas where facts are at odds with most people's intuition, and thus lead many fundraisers to poor decisions:

- *Long fundraising messages.* Who has time for reading long letters or e-mails? Not me. But they work. In direct-mail testing, longer letters usually win. If you want to improve the performance of a direct-mail piece, make the letter longer. It's as dependable as aspirin. Even in e-mail, longer messages often perform better.

- *Frequent fundraising.* There's a destructive myth in our industry that you will increase donor attrition if you communicate too much. The fact is, more frequent fundraising consistently does two things: raises more money and *improves* retention.

---

2. You can't assume everything you hate will automatically be successful. That would be more effective than doing everything you love, but it still isn't smart.

- *Direct mail.* It's not dying, no matter what a hundred bloggers say. It's changing, often becoming part of a two-step, cross-channel response process. But it's still the best fundraising channel there is, after the house-of-worship collection plate. If you abandon direct mail (or avoid it in the first place) you are forgoing a dependable source of income and donor engagement.

Your own mind isn't the only source of nonfacts that can trip you up. Focus groups and surveys can do it, too. They're insidious that way because their findings masquerade as facts; they involve professional rigor. But rigor does not transform an opinion into a fact. It only makes it a more accurately measured opinion.

Focus-group and survey findings are not capable of telling you what your donors are going to do. *They can only tell you what they say.*

Focus-group and survey findings are not capable of telling you what your donors are going to *do*. They can only tell you what they *say*—and what they say in a couple of highly artificial situations.[3] You get *their* opinions, which are no more useful or related to their behavior than are your own opinions.

You can find out many useful things with focus groups and surveys. Mainly, how donors talk about your cause, and what they do or don't grasp. But you can't learn what people will do about your fundraising when it matters.

If you need to know what donors will do (and you very much need to know), you must observe their behavior in real life. What they do at their mailbox or inbox is what you must watch.

---

3. How often do you make decisions while explaining your thinking to a dozen strangers around a table, knowing some weird people are watching you from behind a one-way window?

HOW TO LEARN WHEN YOU'RE TOO SMALL TO TEST

Without disciplined direct-response testing, you don't really know what works in fundraising. But the majority of non-profits have too few donors and operate at too small a scale to get accurate results from testing. In direct mail, you need to be mailing in the tens of thousands or more to get results you can read. In e-mail, add an extra zero to that. Anything smaller will yield statistical noise. You won't learn anything. Worse yet, it may seem that you've learned something when all you have is noise.

That doesn't mean you're left without access to useful knowledge if your numbers are too small for testing. Here are two things you can do:

1. Watch Those Who Do Test

Larger organizations and the agencies and consultants that serve them test constantly. What you see them doing in the marketplace is the product of repeated testing and refining.

Steal from them. You'd be crazy not to. Their testing is your free research and development program.

I often hear this objection to stealing from the testers: *Our donors are different! What works for others won't work for us!*

It's true that your donors and your cause are unique. But probably not as different as you think. Could your donors perform completely differently from the majority of donors? Conceivably, yes. Likely? No.

2. Learn by Trying

Every time you try something different in fundraising, you learn. Make changes consciously and pay close attention to changes in response that follow your changes in approach.

(continued)

For your weakest campaigns, change things freely—especially the fundraising offer. If you do better than you did last year, you most likely have a winner. Be more cautious about changes to your strong campaigns.

Small changes year to year or campaign to campaign are not interesting and less likely repeatable. It's the big changes (for better or worse) that should grab your attention.

Here are some high-impact things you should try, seeking changes for the better:

- Offer.
- Images.
- Significant changes to the physical specification of the package.
- Different copy.
- Changes to the outer envelope (or e-mail subject line).

Don't waste your time on these low-impact areas:

- Color.
- Design changes.
- Minor differences in copy.
- Postage treatments.
- Anything on the back of the reply form.

A DONOR-FOCUSED NONPROFIT DOESN'T TREAT ALL DONORS THE SAME

Imagine your organization has only one donor. His name is William Gates III of Seattle. Think how easy life would be. No guesswork, no mucking around with mail houses. Just one humongous stream of revenue.

That may sound like a dream scenario. Actually, it's more of a nightmare. If Mr. Gates changed his focus, got annoyed with you, or became ill—you'd be in a world of hurt. Your entire public support could be gone in a second.

That's why it's good to have a larger list of donors. When you lose donors (as you inevitably do), you're always replacing them. A change in the life of a donor isn't a catastrophe. As long as your pace of new donor acquisition is enough to keep you from shrinking, you're in good shape.

But having more than one donor means you have people giving different amounts—people of different monetary value to you.

Here's another thought experiment: imagine you have *two* donors—Mr. Gates and Mrs. Calicardia, who sends you a crisp $5 bill every December.

It's easy to see that it would be crazy to spend the same time, energy, and money cultivating each of them. It's a little harder to see this in real life because it's not so binary. Your donors range all the way from the Mrs. Calicardia level to somewhere in the neighborhood of the Mr. Gates level.

The right thing to do is allocate your fundraising resources according to the long-term value of each donor. You should spend more on the larger donors, and you should be stingy with the lower donors.

This can feel a bit antidemocratic or counter to the principle of the Widow's Mite.[4]

But it's a key to success.

Many organizations spend $10 a year cultivating $5-a-year donors. They do that because they're spending the same $10 on everyone who gives $50 and less. The $5 donors are caught up in the crowd. And while those $5 donors are no doubt nice people, they're dragging your fundraising down. That's money you'd be better off spending on donors whose giving justifies it.

All donors are equal as human beings. They are not equal as revenue sources. Treating them as such will cost you, both in wasted spending at the low end and in missed opportunities at the high end.

Look at all your donors by cumulative annual giving. Then make sure you aren't spending too much on the lower donors. ROI should

---

4. Read the very short account in the Gospel of Mark 12:41–44.

be your guide: You can afford to spend more on your higher donors: more contact, more personal touches, more impactful mailings, and acknowledgments.

And you should cut back on contact with the low donors. Not because they'll burn out, but because you will burn out financially if you don't limit your spending on them.

A DONOR-FOCUSED NONPROFIT HAS A CULTURE OF THANKFULNESS

One of the keys to personal happiness is to develop a habit of gratitude. To say *thank you* to others for anything, from small courtesies to their role in your life. To tell yourself and others stories of the good things that have happened to you. To cultivate a sense of conscious thankfulness when good things happen—even to be mindful of the positive that's hidden in bad things that happen to you.

Gratitude can short-circuit our human tendency to focus on the negative and thus create more negativity.

Nonprofit organizations that celebrate gratitude as an organizational trait raise more money, keep donors longer, and create more innovation. They're also better places to work.

A habit of gratitude is even more important for nonprofit organizations. Those that celebrate gratitude as an organizational trait raise more money, keep donors longer, and create more innovation. They're also better places to work.

Fundraising can be tough. But you aren't in it alone, even though it may feel that way at times. You have not only generous donors, but founders, board members, advocates, vendors, and others—all of them critical to your success and continued existence. You should be openly thankful to them all.

Most of all, to donors.

Here are three ways to foster your thankfulness toward donors in the culture of your organization:

1. *Tell stories of donors.* In your employee newsletter, or wherever the real information that people pay attention to is, publish accounts of individual donors who have done great things to help forward your cause. Don't only celebrate the big donors for jaw-dropping largesse. Remember the retired lady in Florida who leaves her air conditioning off to be able to afford an extra gift. Or the kid who sells lemonade all summer and sends you the proceeds. These stories can keep the big souls of donors visible throughout your staff.

2. *Put everyone in contact with donors.* Everyone in the organization should have at least some donor contact. Thanking is a rewarding and eye-opening activity. Spread the joy by giving it to everyone in at least a small way (see Chapter 13).

3. *Be a donor.* Give to your own nonprofit. Give to others. Give by mail. Give online. Give casually to strangers. Study the feeling it creates in you. Study the flood of fundraising that comes your way when you're a donor. You'll discover—with your heart and your head—what donors experience.

A DONOR-FOCUSED NONPROFIT SEES FUNDRAISING AS PART OF ITS MISSION

Your mission—the reason you were founded in the first place—may be only half of the good you're doing in the world. The other half is *your fundraising.*

That may seem like an odd idea, but it's true, whether you embrace it or not. You'll be a better fundraiser when you embrace it.

When you persuade a donor to give, you are not taking something away from her; you are adding grace to her life. Her bank balance may be temporarily lower, but she's meaningfully richer because of the gift. Here are some of the ways giving makes life better:

- Giving helps donors become more evolved, more involved, more connected with the world beyond their immediate circle. Donors care about orphans in Haiti, about endangered animals, about the arts, about medical research. They pay attention to the causes they give to, and that rockets them to the top in all types of awareness and connection. Every time you ask for a gift, you create an opportunity for someone to improve herself.

- Giving increases your donors' happiness and satisfaction with life. If you could watch what happens in a donor's brain when she gives, you'd see the reward centers lighting up like Times Square—the same parts of the brain that are stimulated by food and sex.

- Giving improves donors' physical and mental health. They have a more positive self-assessment, a stronger sense of being in control. They just feel better. Others notice it, too: Donors are more respected by the people around them. There's even evidence that charitable giving improves donors' finances. (The first piece of advice many self-made billionaires give is this: "Start giving away money now!")

- Giving is not only good for donors—it's also good for society. By some estimates, a dollar given to charity stimulates better than $19 for the economy. Beyond that, think of the impact of millions of healthier, more-involved donors.

Fundraising is a win-win-win-win enterprise.

I know it can seem like an endless parade of vexing problems with printing, postal regulations, Web servers, and anything else that can go wrong. But when you remember how much more fundraising is—that it's not just a way to squeeze money out of people's pockets—you can transform your career. And your life.

Of course, we make the world better through the causes we fund. But before that, we help transform our donors.

Donors are people just like you and me. They face health problems and money and job worries. Relationship challenges, sorrow, and pain. Because they're largely older people, they have a lot more to worry about than you and I do.

Your fundraising message reaches through the anxiety and confusion of life. When they make a gift to your organization, they get a little spark of joy and empowerment.

Every day, we have the privilege of being part of the transformation of our donors. If we could see it for what it is, we'd be overcome with wonder. But we can't see it, so we sometimes think all we're doing is just another form of marketing, not meaningfully different from persuading strangers to choose one shampoo over another.

Being mindful of the miracle that fundraising is doesn't keep it from being a pain in the butt. You still don't have the staff and resources you need. Things still go wrong. Your boss, your board, your client, or your consultants still don't get it or get in the way. Great ideas somehow still don't pan out.

But if you keep in mind how much more than marketing you're doing, you'll work with clearer vision. You'll have a better brand. You'll raise more money.

TAKEAWAYS FOR NONPROFIT BRAND BUILDERS

- A donor-focused organization is investment oriented and always seeking improvement.

- A donor-focused organization has a fact-based culture, paying attention to donor behavior over people's opinions and beliefs.

- A donor-focused organization doesn't treat all donors the same. It maximizes ROI by spending enough on higher donors and not too much on lower donors.

- A donor-focused organization has a culture of thankfulness toward all its partners, especially donors.

- A donor-focused organization sees fundraising is part of its mission, as important as its programs.

This book started out with a pessimistic look at what Brand Experts can do to a nonprofit when they bring their ideas to the work. It ends hoping to persuade you that fundraising is the work of angels. In between were a lot of details about how you can avoid the poison pill of corporate-style branding and instead build a brand that connects you with donors.

I hope you can put it to work. I challenge you to make it your goal.

The Donor Bill of Rights and the Money-Raising Brand

The Donor Bill of Rights was created in 1993 by the Association of Fundraising Professionals (AFP), the Association for Healthcare Philanthropy (AHP), and the Council for Advancement and Support of Education (CASE). You'll find that these guidelines require some of the characteristics of a donor-focused brand.

That's why the Donor Bill of Rights can help you improve your brand.

THE DONOR BILL OF RIGHTS

Philanthropy is based on voluntary action for the common good. It is a tradition of giving and sharing that is primary to the quality of life. To ensure that philanthropy merits the respect and trust of the general public, and that donors and prospective donors can have full confidence in the nonprofit organizations and causes they are asked to support, we declare that all donors have these rights:

I. To be informed of the organization's mission, of the way the organization intends to use donated resources, and of its capacity to use donations effectively for their intended purposes.

    Information is the beginning of your connection with donors. When you build your fundraising around clear and specific calls to action, you draw donors in to the core of your work and make them part of it.

II. To be informed of the identity of those serving on the organization's governing board, and to expect the board to exercise prudent judgment in its stewardship responsibilities.

III. To have access to the organization's most recent financial statements.

Few donors care about your board or your financial statements. That doesn't make these things unimportant. Make this information easily available and not obfuscated by legalese.

IV. To be assured their gifts will be used for the purposes for which they were given.

*Any organization with a donor-focused brand will not just **tell** donors their gifts are being put to good use; they'll prove it with well-crafted accounts of what was done with the donor's support.*

V. To receive appropriate acknowledgment and recognition.

No donor should ever wonder if their gift was received or if it mattered to the organization. Prompt and relevant acknowledgment is your first step in building on ongoing relationship with a donor.

VI. To be assured that information about their donation is handled with respect and with confidentiality to the extent provided by law.

More than ever, donors are sensitive about their privacy. More than ever, privacy can be violated even without evil intent—by accident. Make sure your systems are built to protect donor privacy.

VII. To expect that all relationships with individuals representing organizations of interest to the donor will be professional in nature.

VIII. To be informed whether those seeking donations are volunteers, employees of the organization, or hired solicitors.

IX. To have the opportunity for their names to be deleted from mailing lists that an organization may intend to share.

Donors own their own names. Not you.

X.   To feel free to ask questions when making a donation and to receive prompt, truthful, and forthright answers.

Being willing and able to answer questions is a great thing. Even better is to anticipate questions and answer them up front.

APPENDIX B

Suggested Reading for Fundraisers

There are many excellent books that can help you be a better fundraiser. I urge you to read as many of them as possible. I'm including this extremely short reading list because I believe these books can have quick and specific payoff. For each book I've included here, there are several more that belong, even on a short list. But this is a start.

- *Making Money from Donor Newsletters* by Tom Ahern (Emerson & Church, 2013): This is a hands-on resource that will guide you to the best practices for producing a newsletter that does a dual job of improving donor retention by reporting to donors what their gifts accomplish while raising funds by asking effectively. This book is a must for any organization that wants to produce a donor newsletter.

- *Orbiting the Giant Hairball: A Corporate Fool's Guide to Surviving with Grace* by Gordon MacKenzie (Viking, 1998): This is not a fundraising book. But it's easily the best "business" book I've ever read. It's about the awkward reality: We all work within organizations, and organizations by their nature stifle creativity and innovation, even though they desperately need those things. This book shows you how to deal with these realities successfully—how to be useful to and valued by the organization while not being "dragged under" by the unavoidable forces that exist within all organizations.

- *Asking: A 59-Minute Guide to Everything Board Members, Volunteers, and Staff Must Know to Secure the Gift* by Jerold Panas (Emerson & Church, 2002): This classic, probably the best-selling fundraising book of all time, is aimed mainly at people who ask for donations face-to-face. But it's a must-read for all types of fundraisers because it so expertly captures the psychology of asking.

- *How to Write Successful Fundraising Appeals,* 3rd edition, by Mal Warwick (Jossey-Bass, 2013): This is an updated edition of the book that has been the Bible for Fundraisers for many years. This book helped me become a professional. Do not miss this book if you want to succeed!

Index

NOTE: Page references in *italics* refer to exhibits.